An Insider's Guide ON HIRING A BUSINESS ATTORNEY

And How to Make the Relationship Work

John L. Watkins

Published by Ocelot Atlanta LLC, Atlanta, GA

This is a book about how to hire a business attorney. The book gives several illustrations of how the failure to use a business attorney can lead to trouble later. These examples are illustrative and ***do not constitute legal advice.*** The law varies from jurisdiction to jurisdiction, and the examples may not apply to you or your company and may not be correct under the law of your jurisdiction. ***This book does not create an attorney/client relationship between the author and any reader. You should always consult with a competent attorney licensed in your jurisdiction.***

This book makes reference to publications and websites of other authors and companies. No rights are claimed with respect to the publications, content, copyrighted material, trademarks, trade names, service marks or intellectual property rights of third-party authors, companies, and service providers. All third-party authors, companies, and service providers are responsible for their content and publications, including, but not limited to, their rankings and evaluations of individual attorneys and law firms.

This book is meant as a general guide on how to find a business attorney. It is meant to point the reader to tools and techniques that have proven useful to the author in evaluating and engaging attorneys. The author's views are matters of honest *opinion,* but the views of others may differ. The information regarding the tools is believed in good faith to be accurate as of the date of writing, January 2010, but there is always the possibility of errors. In addition, the publications and websites referred to in this book are dynamic and changing. A user should always check for updates on the methods and content of any publication or website before proceeding. This book cannot be a substitute for the user's judgment. The user is solely responsible for any decision made in hiring an attorney. Any attorney engaged is solely responsible for any legal services that may be provided to a user.

ISBN: 1450546730
ISBN-13: 9781450546737

TABLE OF CONTENTS

ABOUT THE AUTHOR

John L. Watkins is a business litigation and business attorney from Atlanta, Georgia. After practicing for almost twenty-five years in a large law firm environment, first Hansell & Post (now Jones, Day), and then McKenna Long & Aldridge, John left McKenna Long in March 2007 for the more entrepreneurial field of "small law." John is currently a shareholder of Chorey, Taylor & Feil, a highly respected small firm in the Buckhead area of Atlanta composed of attorneys formerly at big firms.

Much of John's practice over the years has been in the area of litigation, or, as John puts it, the "sanitation service" end of the law business. John currently concentrates on handling trade secret, insurance coverage, corporate, LLC, and commercial contract disputes. However, in over twenty-seven years of practicing, John has handled most types of business litigation matters, including product liability, construction, securities, and other matters.

John also handles general business matters for a number of clients, including reviewing and negotiating their sales contracts, nondisclosure agreements, and terms and conditions. Much of John's current work involves assisting clients with strategies to avoid getting into disputes, or to resolve them outside of the court system.

Although John's practice is based in Georgia, he has handled particular litigation matters in the courts of many other states, including New York, California, Florida, Arizona, Virginia, Missouri, Colorado, Arkansas, Michigan, and Delaware, and has supervised or coordinated the handling of litigation matters in other states. He also handles business matters that involve interacting with attorneys in other states and sometimes other countries.

Because of the nature of his practice, John often has occasion to interview and engage attorneys in other jurisdictions on behalf of his clients. John has worked with many businesses, large, medium and small. Many of John's clients are international companies or their U.S. subsidiaries. John is active in the German American Chamber of Commerce, the British American Business Group, and other international trade and business organizations in Atlanta.

John was named to the list of Georgia "Super Lawyers" published by *Atlanta Magazine* and *Law and Politics* in the field of business litigation for 2008, 2009, and 2010. In 2010, John was listed in the top 100 Super Lawyers in Georgia based on the highest point totals in the Georgia nomination, research, and review process. For many years, John has been rated "AV" by the *Martindale-Hubbell* law directory, its highest rating. John is rated 10.0 by AVVO, its highest rating. John was on the Board of Directors of the Atlanta Bar Association's Construction Section from 2005 to 2009, and served two stints on the Board of Directors at McKenna Long & Aldridge. He is a Master in the Bleckley Inn of Court, an organization that allows experienced attorneys to interact with younger attorneys from other firms and law students from the Georgia State University School of Law. In addition to being an attorney, John is a registered mediator.

John has written many articles about legal issues. He has spoken at many seminars and conferences on legal topics such as trade secrets and nondisclosure agreements, product liability, arbitration and mediation, including before the International Chamber of Commerce (IHK) in Munich, Germany; the Center for International Legal Studies in Heidelberg, Germany; the German American Chamber of Commerce in Atlanta; the Institute for Continuing Legal Education in Atlanta and Athens, Georgia; and the Atlanta Bar Association Construction and Alternative Dispute Resolution Sections.

John attended the University of Georgia School of Law, where he graduated first in his class in 1982. He was awarded the Order of the Coif, the Jessie and Dan MacDougald Award, the Isaac Meinhard Award, the Class of 1933 Torts Award, and other awards. He was on the *Georgia Law Review*, and was a member of the Intrastate Trial Team. While in law school John served as a research assistant and teaching assistant in the business school, and co-authored (with Professor O. Lee Reed) one of the first scholarly articles making the case for product liability tort reform. That article was published in the *Nebraska Law Review.* John also received a full academic scholarship.

John lives with his wife Margaret in the Atlanta metropolitan area. He is a frustrated golfer and an amateur photographer. He blogs about legal topics at http://www.ctflegal.blogspot.com, podcasts on legal issues at http://http://www.ctflegal.blip.tv (also available for free at the iTunes store by searching for "ctflegal"), and is recognized as an expert author at http://www.ezinearticles.com.

ACKNOWLEDGMENTS AND DEDICATION

It is impossible to achieve success in any profession or endeavor without the assistance of others. So many people have contributed to my career that I am hesitant to mention anyone for fear of omitting others equally deserving of mention. With that reservation, I would first like to thank the University of Georgia School of Law for providing me with an excellent legal education.

Thanks also go out to my colleagues at Hansell & Post (now the Atlanta office of Jones, Day) for helping me lay the foundation in the real world of practicing law. Special thanks from those days go to the late Jule W. Felton, Jr., who was kind enough to offer me a job and let me handle work early on for his best client, the late Hugh M. Dorsey, Jr., who taught me a lot about practicing law and not a little about living a good life, David J. Bailey, who took the time to help me "get it" (I will always be grateful), W. Rhett Tanner, who was willing to give me as much rope as I could handle, Richard M. Kirby, who was always tough but stood up for me, and John G. Parker, an outstanding litigator. Many thanks as well to my contemporaries, all of whom have gone on to great success. It was a great place to start.

After a little more than four years at Hansell & Post, I followed some colleagues to Long, Aldridge & Norman, which later became McKenna Long & Aldridge LLP. There were so many great colleagues over the years at this firm, but Jack Watson should be singled out as an early mentor. Phil Bradley deserves special recognition as a mentor, but also as a friend. Phil, I miss the old days sometimes. I will always respect you. Chuck Reed, what can I say? I learned a lot from you and I hope you learned a little from me. Anyway, we had a good time, and I hope there will be more. A different kind of thanks goes out to Russ Rogers, who was my number one associate before he made partner and made his own mark. Thanks for all your great work Russ, but I learned a lot from you as well, and you have been a great friend. There are so many others who could be mentioned, and I think you know who you are. Thanks to all of you.

After deciding to enter "small law" in 2007, special thanks must go out to Mike Rosenthal, of Wagner, Johnston & Rosenthal. Mike has been a great friend for many years and is a great lawyer. I'm glad we practiced together for a short while. At my current firm, Tom Chorey is an inspiration who sets a very high standard in terms of quality, enthusiasm, and work habits. Tom is the only person I freely concede I cannot out work.

In terms of preparing this book, the views and opinions are mine alone. However, it would be very remiss not to mention Shelly Shepard, owner of The Final Word in Charlotte, North Carolina, who provided excellent copyediting and proofreading assistance. Thanks for your good work, Shelly.

Finally, thanks for many great years to my spouse, Margaret. This book is dedicated to you. It is not easy being a business litigator's wife, as late arrivals from the office are the norm, travel can be frequent, and many nights and weekends are spent alone. It takes a strong person to deal with this generally, not to mention an even stronger person to tolerate my personal foibles and limitations. I'm not sure why you stuck with it, but I'm sure glad you did.

John L. Watkins
Atlanta, Georgia
January 2010

IMPORTANT DISCLAIMER

What I am about to say is obvious, but probably needs to be said anyway. This book is meant as a general guide on how to find a business attorney and how to make the relationship work. It will point you to tools and techniques that have proven useful to me in evaluating and engaging attorneys. My views are matters of honest *opinion,* but the views of others may differ.

The book gives several illustrations of how the failure to use a business attorney can lead to trouble later. These examples are illustrative and ***do not constitute legal advice.*** The law varies from jurisdiction to jurisdiction, and the examples may not apply to you or your company and may not be correct under the law of your jurisdiction. ***This book does not create an attorney/client relationship between the author and any reader. You should always consult with a competent attorney licensed in your jurisdiction (this is one of the main points of the book).***

The information regarding the tools referred to in this book -- other publications and websites -- is believed in good faith to be accurate as of the date of writing, January 2010, but there ***is always the possibility of errors.*** In addition, the publications and websites referred to in this book are ***dynamic and changing.*** Readers should always check for updates on the methods and content of any publication or website before using any tool referred to in this book. ***The authors and publishers of the tools are solely responsible for their content, including their rankings of attorneys and law firms.***

This book cannot be a substitute for the reader's judgment. ***The reader or user is solely responsible for any decision to hire any particular*** *attorney. Any attorney engaged is solely responsible for any legal services that may be provided to a reader or the reader's business.*

By proceeding to use the book, each reader is agreeing he understands and is bound by the disclosures, warnings, and limitations stated herein.

INTRODUCTION

I have practiced law for over 27 years, most of which have been in a big firm environment. In early 2007, I decided to change to a smaller firm. Much of my practice has been in the field of business litigation, or, as some would call it, the "sanitation service" end of the law. For the most part, we clean up (or try to clean up) the messes that businesses or individuals find themselves in by fighting it out in court, or through alternative dispute methods such as mediation and arbitration. Sanitation service in the legal profession can be a very expensive proposition.

Having handled many types of cases for a variety of companies in assorted venues, I have always been struck by one common thread: A surprising number of disputes and issues could have been avoided entirely if the business *had simply obtained competent legal help on the front end* – that is, help in forming a business, drafting a contract, or generally handling its business affairs. Many other disputes might not have been avoided, but, again with proper legal help on the front end, could have been resolved more efficiently and quickly and for far less money.

The root cause of such issues is typically quite easy to ascertain. Perhaps the most common cause is that the company did not use a lawyer at all, thinking it could get by with a homemade contract, a form pulled off the Internet, or by trying to reuse a legal document from a prior transaction without legal help. Another cause is that the company, perhaps hungry for business, signed a contract or form prepared by the other side and, in so doing, signed away all its rights. Another cause is that the company has a lawyer, but does not follow advice, or conducts its business in a manner contrary to the terms and conditions the lawyer painstakingly prepared. Finally, but far less often, the company had a lawyer, but the lawyer simply did not do a good job.

Millions, if not hundreds of millions, of dollars are spent each year to try to clean up such messes. And "try" is the operative word because the sanitation service does not come with a guarantee. Many legal messes simply cannot be easily resolved.

In thinking about these issues, it dawned on me that many business executives simply do not know how to find a good lawyer. Oh sure, they may meet many lawyers at business events or cocktail parties, but how do you tell a good one from a not-so-good one? Or, they may find the prospect of dealing with lawyers daunting. Or the fees. How do lawyers charge, anyway? If you hire one, how do you work with a lawyer effectively?

This guide will give you inside information on all of these issues. It is going to provide you with the tools you need to find a good business lawyer and to work with a lawyer in a mutually beneficial way. Once you find the right person, your business lawyer should become a trusted adviser and resource for your business, a resource that will help keep your company out of trouble and actually save it money in the long run.

CHAPTER 1:
WHY DO I NEED A BUSINESS ATTORNEY, ANYWAY?

"The first thing we do, let's kill all the lawyers."

-William Shakespeare, *Henry VI*, Part 2 (Act IV, Scene II)

It is hardly a secret that my profession is not held in wide esteem by much of the public. It is certainly true that some attorneys have not covered themselves (or the profession) with glory. Some people may have a generally negative attitude toward all attorneys because they believe that a single sharp or sleazy attorney took advantage of them, a friend or a relative in a legal matter.

If you have purchased this book, however, you are probably convinced you need a business attorney and want to know how to find a good one who can become a trusted adviser and part of your company's inner circle. That said, some may still require a little convincing. Allow me to make the case.

The Prime Directive. This short paragraph alone is worth the price of this book, which is why it is called the "Prime Directive." There are very few absolute truths in the legal profession. For every legal rule, there is at least one exception. There is one rule, however, that is pretty close to universally true: *It is almost always more effective and less expensive to involve a lawyer earlier in the process than later.* In other words, it is almost always less expensive to deal with an issue immediately

– such as by making sure a contract is properly drafted – than trying to resolve or litigate a business dispute that may arise later.

Over the years, the failure of businesses and individuals to follow the Prime Directive has kept me and many other litigation attorneys in business. The examples alone could fill a book. Here are a few.

Corporate and company formation issues. There are few things sadder than an initial meeting with a client who has worked years to build a business only to find that he or she does not actually control the business. How does this happen? Today, it is extremely easy and inexpensive to form a business, and companies can be formed in many ways without the involvement of lawyers. Sometimes, the founder's accountant will form the business. Accountants seem to be viewed by many business people as a necessity and lawyers as a luxury. This approach often proves to be an expensive mistake in the long run.

For the adventurous, there are also Internet companies that will form a corporation or limited liability company (LLC) for very low fees. Just have the accountant or Internet company fill out the forms (or do it yourself), send them in to the appropriate state office (usually the Secretary of State) with the appropriate fee, and you have created a new legal entity. What could go wrong?

Many things can go wrong. In the past twenty years, LLCs have become a popular form of entity because they are very flexible and generally provide for "flow through" taxation, meaning that profits in the business are not taxed at the company level and then again when distributions are made to the owners. Instead, the tax liability flows through to the owners, thus avoiding "double taxation."

In Georgia, where I practice, an LLC can be formed with a simple two or three-page filing. What if, for example, you contribute all of the capital to start an LLC and fund its operations with additional cash infusions until it is profitable. However, perhaps you have a colleague who started the business with you, and you want to award that person a 10 percent equity interest as "sweat equity." Accordingly, when the business is formed, you list yourself and the colleague as the "members" of the LLC.

Several years later, when the business is profitable and you want to sell the business or some dispute has developed between you and the colleague, you finally consult a lawyer. Your nasty surprise will be that, unless you properly documented the members' rights (relative ownership, voting and distribution rights) in an operating agreement, Georgia law provides that you and your colleague are equal participants, with equal rights to vote, manage the business and receive profits.

You can imagine the plethora of legal problems that this can create. Fixing this problem on the back end, if it is possible, will require the cooperation and good faith of the other member, first, to stick to the unwritten understanding, and, second, to fix it with proper documentation. Human nature being what it is, your colleague may not agree to this after discovering his or her legal interests.

All of this could have been avoided if you had paid a business lawyer a small fee to draw up an operating agreement when the business was formed. At that time, the other participant would have been delighted to sign an operating agreement as a minority participant because it would have been, so to speak, "found money."

As another example, your accountant may advise you to set up the business as a subchapter S corporation (actually, a tax election) because it also allows "flow through" taxation. This is certainly a good choice for many businesses. However, there are limitations on who can own stock in such corporations. Generally, stock ownership is restricted to individuals who are U.S. citizens.

If your concept is to build a business and then sell it to investors, a subchapter S election may not be the best choice, as it will limit the number of potential investors. It is certainly true that a good corporate attorney with a tax background (working with a company's accountants) can probably find a way to structure a buyout. However, it may come with some adverse tax consequences that simply cannot be avoided. Again, some planning on the front end might save a lot of money on the back end.

These examples alone should be enough to convince you that using a business attorney is a good idea when starting a business. As always, the above examples may not apply to you (because of differences in state law, changes in the law, or particular circumstances). The examples, however, illustrate the fundamental point: Starting a business without good legal advice can result in expensive consequences that could have been avoided with a little planning.

Contracts, and terms and conditions. Over the years, I have litigated countless contract disputes. Many of these disputes have involved limited documentation (such as a "naked" purchase order), no documentation, or "homemade" contracts. Sometimes the documentation is so scant or vague that I have literally had to ask a client – now faced with litigation or at least the prospect of it – "What exactly were you trying to accomplish in this transaction?"

It goes without saying that, if a party's lawyer cannot figure out what the parties were trying to document, there is a pretty good chance that a court will not do much better. Unless reason prevails on the other side and a quick settlement is reached, these circumstances usually lead to litigation and to a very uncertain result. Court proceedings always carry a risk of an adverse outcome, and, when a court has little to go on, the level of uncertainty increases exponentially.

The homemade contract creates particular problems. Many business people assume that, since they were capable enough of starting a business and (hopefully) making money from it, they are capable of drawing up a simple contract. In fairness, a lawyer will occasionally see a homemade contract that is pretty good and actually accomplishes the objective. More often than not, however, they are a disaster. Why is this the case?

One reason homemade contracts tend to be a disaster is that business people often greatly overestimate their ability to write clearly. Some of the best business people are, to put it bluntly, functionally illiterate on paper. Even if a person can write clearly, documenting a business agreement is a much different proposition than, for example, writing a letter, a business proposal, or marketing materials.

Another reason business people are typically not adept at writing contracts is that they are not used to writing agreements from an *objective* perspective. Most people have been in situations where they have an understanding with another person but have difficulty explaining the transaction to a third person. Business lawyers are usually able to distill the parties' "deal" into a document understandable by third parties.

Documenting the agreement objectively is extremely important because, in the event of a dispute, a court will look to the written agreement of the parties as the embodiment of the contract. As a general proposition, the law uses the "objective theory of contracts," meaning that the court will look to how the parties embodied the contract, not to unstated subjective intentions of a party. If a written contract is clear, particularly in a commercial setting, courts will, in the vast majority of instances, simply enforce it.

If a contract is unclear, however, a court may determine in extreme circumstances that, whatever may have been intended, the contract is just too vague to be enforced. In most circumstances, however, a court will first apply rules of construction, which are legal maxims that are used to interpret a contract. The court may also look to industry usage of words and custom and practice in the industry. If the contract remains unclear, the court may hear "parol evidence," or evidence outside of the contract, to determine what it means. All of the foregoing ultimately means that the result is dependent on how the court sees things, which may be very different from your understanding.

A professionally drafted contract will provide a much greater chance of a result consistent with your understanding in the event of a dispute after the contract is signed. However, an even greater benefit is that a well-drafted contract will prevent many disputes from ever developing. The process of negotiating a contract and reaching an agreement with the other side will often bring differences in understandings to the surface. Further discussion and negotiation can bridge those differences.

I remember one contract from many years ago that was a particularly tough negotiation. The other side was extremely demanding, often to the point of being unreasonable. Many times during the negotiations I thought the transaction had fallen apart. I even counseled my client that, if the other side was so unreasonable in negotiations, it might well be equally unreasonable in performing the contract, and I questioned whether we should consider not concluding the deal. At the end of the day, however, we were able to hammer out a very detailed agreement. My client later told me that the project had proceeded as smoothly as any he had ever been involved in; if a question arose, the parties simply consulted the contract and abided by its terms. All of the effort negotiating the contract proved its worth.

There is another way that a well-drafted contract can prevent disputes. If a potential dispute later develops, the other party will probably consult a lawyer. If that lawyer reviews the contract and informs the other side that there is nothing there, a lawsuit may again be avoided. Most lawyers (and, I admit, not all lawyers) do not want to take a case they are unlikely to win.

Although having a clear contract is reason enough to engage a lawyer to draft a business contract, other reasons exist as well. Many business people – and particularly sales people – do not understand that their actions may have unintended legal consequences. For example, if you sell products, you may employ a sales force trained to act as consultants for customers. Sales people may meet with customers, assess their needs, and prepare proposals. Proposals may contain cost-saving or labor-saving analyses, often in considerable detail.

There is probably no doubt that such selling techniques can be extremely effective. However, they may legally create binding warranty obligations. Many business people are surprised to find out that a warranty may be created outside of a sales contract or formal warranty document. However, under the Uniform Commercial Code, or UCC (which applies in Georgia and quite universally throughout the United States), an "express" warranty can be created by any affirmation of fact about the product that is part of the basis of the bargain. Statements of general commendation, however, are considered to be sales talk or "puffing" and do not create express warranties.

If the product does not conform to the salesperson's representations and analyses, it is possible that your company will face a return, or worse, a lawsuit, based on breach of express warranty. If that were not enough, the UCC also can operate to create an "implied warranty of fitness for a particular purpose." This implied warranty arises when the buyer is relying on the seller's expertise to furnish a suitable product for the buyer's needs. In such a circumstance, the failure of a product to conform to the buyer's needs can be a breach of this implied warranty. Again, if a salesperson is acting as a consultant, an implied warranty of fitness for a particular purpose is likely to arise.

In addition to express warranties and the implied warranty of fitness for a particular purpose, the UCC creates an "implied warranty of merchantability." The implied warranty of merchantability essentially provides that goods are of fair, average quality and generally suitable for their intended use.

Implied warranty claims present particular problems because they are based on vague and general standards. As such, an implied warranty claim is often bounded only by the creativity of the claimant's counsel. Trust me, many lawyers can be quite creative in pressing claims!

A good business lawyer can substantially reduce the risk of warranty claims through contractual terms. Implied warranties can usually be disclaimed, but doing so effectively requires use of particular language. Express warranty issues can be dealt with by making the written contract and its terms (including any warranties in the contract) the entire and only agreement between the parties. ***Important note:*** Warranty issues, like all legal issues, can vary among states. Additional issues can arise if you are selling consumer products. So, as always, consult with an attorney in your jurisdiction regarding your particular circumstances.

Intellectual Property. Many business people think of intellectual property as patents, copyrights and trademarks. Most businesses probably do not maintain a portfolio of such items, and, if they do, already utilize legal counsel. However, almost all businesses have some form of confidential or proprietary information that is a key to their competitive edge. Examples include customer lists, supplier lists, production techniques, formulas, databases or computer programs.

Even though such information may be the lifeblood of the company, many business people do not pay much attention to such information until a key employee walks off with copies and starts a competing business. At that time, the business owner may visit a litigation attorney. The first question will be whether the employee had signed a non-disclosure agreement ("NDA"), also known as a confidentiality agreement. If the answer is "no," the chances of obtaining redress are reduced.

In Georgia, for example, confidential and proprietary information may rise to the level of a trade secret, in which case it is protected by the state trade secret statute. If information does not rise to the level of a trade secret, it is subject to protection under an NDA. If the departing employee has not signed an NDA, it may still be possible to obtain relief under a trade secrets statute or possibly other theories of liability.

However, in order to qualify as a trade secret, information has to meet certain statutory requirements, one of which is typically that the information was subject to reasonable efforts to keep it confidential. It is much easier to meet this requirement if the information has been subject to an NDA. In addition, a consultation with a business attorney, often in conjunction with the client's information technology officer, can develop other methods that will protect confidential information and preserve possible legal remedies.

Internet forms and "leftovers." Many businesses know they need proper legal protection but feel they must save money, perhaps because of the current difficult economic climate. They are tempted, therefore, to pull free forms off of the Internet or to buy forms from a legal document service. They may also be tempted to recycle forms used on other projects, perhaps even forms that were prepared by the other side in an earlier business transaction.

Using Internet forms and leftovers from prior transactions can be a risky proposition. The problem is that business people lack the legal training to tailor the forms to the needs of the particular circumstances. For example, the form may have been developed for the law of another state. Similarly, a form sales agreement developed for a seller will rarely be appropriate for a buyer. By using such forms and not having a full understanding of the issues, businesses may be giving up important legal rights. In any event, it would be pure happenstance if such an approach resulted in an optimal agreement.

It is true that lawyers often create documents by using forms or clauses they have developed in prior transactions. The difference is that a lawyer will know whether a document is, for example, meant to protect a buyer or a seller. Even relatively simple business documents, such as NDAs, can have important differences designed to protect the disclosing party or designed to limit the responsibility of the receiving party. The lawyer will tailor the documents to the needs of the client and the particular transaction. The lawyer will probably also develop entirely new provisions drafted exclusively for the particular transaction.

If you were not already convinced when you bought this book, hopefully these examples have demonstrated why you need a good business attorney. It should be stressed that, although the examples are relatively common ones, there are many other reasons why you should regularly consult with counsel. Now that you are convinced, we will turn to finding the right attorney for your business.

Chapter 1 Summary

- The "Prime Directive": It is almost always more effective and less expensive to involve a lawyer earlier in the process than later.
- Using an Internet service or homemade document to form a corporation or LLC can have unexpected and costly consequences.
- Homemade legal contracts are risky because they will probably not clearly and objectively document the transaction.
- Common sales techniques can have unintended consequences, such as creating warranties.
- Proper contract language can substantially reduce the risk of making unintended warranties and avoiding other unintended consequences.
- Failing to use properly developed nondisclosure agreements and developing procedures to protect proprietary information create unnecessary business risks.
- Using Internet forms and reusing "leftovers" is no substitute for professional advice.
- These are only some examples of why you need a business lawyer.

CHAPTER 2: RESOURCES FOR FINDING A GOOD BUSINESS ATTORNEY

"In a time of turbulence and change, it is more true than ever that knowledge is power . . ."

-John F. Kennedy,
Address at University of California at Berkeley, March 23, 1962

Background Considerations

Even many relatively sophisticated business people seem to think that attorneys are fungible, meaning that one attorney can do whatever another attorney can do. After all, we all went to law school and took pretty much the same curriculum. We all passed a bar exam and other requirements to practice law, and we are all licensed to practice in one or more states. This view reflects a lack of knowledge. This chapter will direct you to the resources that will enable you to gather considerable information about lawyers in your community.

Although all lawyers share the common characteristics noted above, please be assured that all lawyers are not equal in their talents, and they are certainly not fungible. To begin with, whether by design or happenstance, most lawyers have some degree of specialization. This book is about hiring and working with business attorneys. To that end, we can exclude from consideration criminal law attorneys, divorce and family law attorneys, plaintiff's personal injury attorneys, insurance defense attorneys, trust and estate attorneys, government contract attorneys, labor law attorneys, and government attorneys from consideration. To be sure, many fine attorneys work in each of these and other areas of the law. Our search, however, is for a business attorney.

Business attorneys tend to fall into two general groups: corporate attorneys and commercial litigators. As a general proposition, corporate attorneys are involved in setting up corporations and LLCs, drafting commercial contracts, and handling mergers and acquisitions. Commercial litigators handle disputes, traditionally, civil lawsuits. In this day and age, however, commercial litigators advise on resolving disputes prior to litigation and will often be familiar with "alternative dispute resolution," which includes mediation and arbitration.

In some instances, a business lawyer will handle aspects of both the traditional corporate and litigation practice. Some lawyers will do this from the outset, but it would be very unusual in a large firm environment. Other lawyers may have their practice shift from one area to the other. As a general proposition, it would probably be more common for a commercial litigator to begin handling aspects of corporate law than it would be for a corporate lawyer to begin handling litigation.

My practice, for example, started out many years ago as a purely commercial litigation practice. Gradually, I began negotiating and drafting sales contracts, terms and conditions, nondisclosure agreements, and other aspects of corporate law. Although I still consider myself primarily a litigator, the other business aspects of my practice are important. I have seen other commercial litigators take a similar path, and, although I might be biased, I believe that a good commercial litigator can serve very well as a client's main business attorney. There will be more on this subject later in the book.

It may be surprising to readers to know that lawyers probably have more experience in hiring other lawyers than most business executives. For example, I have often had to hire "local counsel" to assist in handling lawsuits. Although most lawyers are licensed in only one state (some are licensed in two or more), it is possible to handle litigation in other jurisdictions by being admitted "*pro hac vice*," which means being admitted to handle a single case and not to practice generally. It is invariably a legal requirement and a practical necessity to engage local counsel to assist.

I have seen a number of other litigators use local counsel purely as a "mail drop," meaning that they want to use local counsel only to comply with the legal requirements and to maintain control of the case themselves. In my view, this is a mistake, as two heads are usually better than one, and having competent co-counsel familiar with the judge and the local community is by far the best alternative for the client. Thus, I always try to engage the best local counsel available to assist.

In addition, I have also assisted clients with nonlitigation matters in other jurisdictions. This has most typically been for international clients or their U.S. subsidiaries. Again, the task is the same: Find the best available local counsel to assist.

Another way that lawyers become involved in evaluating other lawyers is through hiring decisions. Over the years, I have interviewed scores of law students and lawyers wanting to join my firm. The process is essentially the same as evaluating local counsel: Considering their qualifications and whether they will fit in with the team.

Your Goal

After following the process in this chapter and Chapter 3, your ultimate goal is to identify at least three lawyers from three law firms as candidates to be your company's primary business attorney. Your list may contain more than three, but you should try to have at least three to provide for a reasonable final evaluation. You will then interview the candidates using the information you have gathered and the interviewing techniques discussed later in the book. From this process, you should have one or more candidates to pick as your primary business attorney.

However, you need to begin at the beginning, and you first need to develop a larger list from which the final candidates will be selected. Logically, the approach should be like a funnel: Start with a larger group and then winnow it down based on your company's needs and the attorney's qualifications. This chapter will discuss the resources available to compile a fairly comprehensive list of candidates for possible inclusion on your final list.

If you already have some knowledge of the legal community, it may provide you with a bit of a leg up in the process. It will be interesting for you to see whether what you think you know measures up with the information you will gather from the resources.

In using the resources, you will want to consider the geographic reach of your search. If you live in a small community, you may want to include lawyers from the nearest city in your search. Please note that I am not suggesting that you may not find the perfect attorney in your community. Having handled many matters in smaller cities and towns, I can assure you that there are many sophisticated and capable lawyers in smaller communities. In addition, many local legal matters effectively require local representation.

This book, however, is about selecting your primary business attorney. There will be a smaller number of lawyers to choose from in a small town, which correspondingly decreases the chances of finding the right person. Only you can judge your situation, but, if you are in a small town or city, you may want to consider expanding the geographic scope of your search.

What Information to Collect

As you use the resources discussed below, you will want to act in a systematic way to collect information. As you make your list, collect the following information on attorneys. You may wish to create a simple spreadsheet or table for this purpose and update it as you go through the process outlined in this and the following chapters.

- Name, firm name, address, telephone number, fax number and e-mail address.
- Year admitted to practice.
- Law school attended, year of graduation, and any honors. Designations for honors vary between schools, but typically include designations such as summa cum laude, magna cum laude, cum laude, "with honors," and "with distinction."
- Law school activities. Important activities may include participation on the school's main law review or journal or participation in a secondary journal (such as a journal covering a more specific area, such as international law). If a person was an editor of a law review or journal, note that fact. Other activities may include representing the school on moot court or trial competition teams.
- Law school scholarships and awards. Make note of any academic scholarships or awards received. Awards vary among law schools. You may see references to "*American Jurisprudence* Book Awards." These are given to the student

making the highest grade in a particular subject, such as a contracts or torts class.

- Judicial clerkships. Federal and state court judges hire law clerks, most often out of law school, to assist them. Most clerkships last one or two years. Clerkships are generally considered prestigious positions. If a lawyer had a clerkship, note the court and the length of the clerkship.
- Awards or designations as a practicing lawyer. Various designations and awards are given to practicing lawyers. Examples include being rated AV® by *Martindale-Hubbell® Law Directory,* receiving a high rating by AVVO™, being named to the "*Super Lawyers*®" list, and being listed in publications such as *Chambers* or *Best Lawyers® in America.* These awards and designations will be discussed below. Make note of any awards or designations received.
- Referrals and recommendations. Note any pertinent referrals or recommendations by clients or other lawyers. Make note of any reasons given for the referral.
- Expertise in your area of business. If a lawyer has any particular expertise relevant to your area of business or industry, make note of the fact and summarize the experience.
- Articles or writing. Make note of any articles or writing, particularly if they appear to relate to your business or industry.
- Public speaking and presentations. Note any public speaking or presentations of interest. Lawyers are asked to speak on topics more often if they are considered to possess particular knowledge of the subject.

It will be rare that you will find information on each of the foregoing subjects for each lawyer. That is to be expected, so just note what applies. You may also not want to spend the time digging for in-depth information for each candidate, particularly at this early stage. Although I urge you to be as thorough as possible, at least gather information on a candidate's law school, law school honors, law school activities, and awards and designations as a practicing attorney. The following section will discuss the resources available to gather this information.

Resources

Local referrals and recommendations. If you know other business people in the community, you may wish to ask them for referrals and recommendations regarding good business law firms and business lawyers in the community. Although you will want to compile these recommendations, you will also want to take them with a grain of salt because you cannot be sure whether the recommendation is an informed one. If you meet lawyers with other specialties in the community, such as a trust and estates lawyer, a divorce lawyer, or an environmental lawyer, you may wish to ask them for recommendations.

Martindale-Hubbell Law Directory. For many years, *Martindale-Hubbell* was the primary resource for finding lawyers. It consists of a large, multi-volume set of books in which attorneys are listed by the city and state in which their office is located. Before the Internet, the standard way to find a lawyer in another jurisdiction was to go to the *Martindale-Hubbell* directory, pull down the applicable volume, turn to the city and study the results. The directory has profiles of most of the firms. It is easy to tell which of the firms are the largest in the city or town. The directory also has short profiles on individual lawyers.

Martindale-Hubbell also has ratings of firms and lawyers. Traditionally, these ratings have been AV ("preeminent"), then BV® and then CV®. However, *Martindale-Hubbell* has recently revamped its ratings somewhat and has now eliminated the CV rating, replacing it with the notation that an attorney is "rated." It should be noted that many lawyers are not rated at all, which means that *Martindale-Hubbell* had not received enough feedback to rate them.

In terms of using *Martindale-Hubbell*, my view is that there is still value to pulling down the print volume and looking at it. It provides a quick, but quite thorough, overview of a city's or town's legal community. The print volumes are usually available in law school libraries, public law libraries, and in some general public libraries.

If you cannot find the print volumes, however, *Martindale-Hubbell* is available online at http://www.martindale.com® and its sister website http://www.lawyers.com℠. These sites can be useful in locating lawyers, but, in a large city, can produce an overwhelming number of results. Both sites sell placement ads for particular categories of the law. In other words, a law firm can pay to appear on a page by buying advertising. Accordingly, you should not assume that the fact that a firm appears on a page or at the top of a page means anything one way or the other as to the firm's capabilities.

In Chapter 3, there will be further observations about how to use the *Martindale-Hubbell* ratings. For the purposes of developing your initial list, just record whether a lawyer is rated or not, and, if the lawyer is rated, make a note of the rating.

AVVO. AVVO is a new service, found at http://www.avvo.com, which maintains rankings of lawyers in most states. AVVO maintains rankings of lawyers on a 10-point scale, with 10 being the best. AVVO initially publishes information on lawyers from publicly available sources (such as state bar registries). The initial listings tend to be quite spare. A lawyer may then claim his profile, which is basically like registering for a social networking site such as LinkedIn. After registering, a lawyer may add considerable additional information, such as a photograph, educational background, awards, bar activities, publications, and speaking engagements.

Adding information can dramatically affect a lawyer's ranking on AVVO. Having observed this process for myself and several other lawyers in our firm, it appears that AVVO will often rank an experienced lawyer around 6.5 based on the basic public information it has gathered. Sometimes a lawyer will have no rating and simply a designation of "no concern." This means that AVVO has found no disciplinary violations by the lawyer but does not have enough information for a ranking. As information is added, AVVO's algorithm will often make the ranking dramatically higher. If a lawyer has taken the time to fill out his or her AVVO profile, it may contain extremely useful information regarding the lawyer's background. For example, I basically use my AVVO profile as a place to store most of my biographical background.

There will be more discussion of the AVVO ratings in Chapter 3. For present purposes, however, if you find a possible candidate, note whether it appears the lawyer has claimed his or her profile. If a lawyer appears to have claimed the profile (meaning it has more than just bare bones information) and is rated, make a note of the rating. If a lawyer does not appear to have claimed the profile or is simply not rated, make a note of that fact.

Chambers & Partners. *Chambers* publishes a legal guide that is based on law firm submissions, client interviews, and database research. *Chambers* started in the United Kingdom and has traditionally focused on law firms with international practices. *Chambers* now publishes a guide to U.S. lawyers. More information is available at http://www.chambersandpartners.com. The U.S. Guide is available for purchase on the *Chambers* website for £130. In addition, the website has a free searchable database.

There will be more on *Chambers* in Chapter 3. For now, if you find a lawyer who is listed in *Chambers*, make a note of the fact.

Super Lawyers. *Super Lawyers* was started by *Law and Politics* and publishes lists of lawyers in various regional publications designated as "Super Lawyers." *Super Lawyers* does not cover all states. *Super Lawyers* surveys lawyers and also states that it has its own independent evaluation process. *Super Lawyers* states that its process results in listing only up to 5 percent of the lawyers in a state. *Super Lawyers* designates lawyers in different categories. *Super Lawyers* has a searchable database at http://www.superlawyers.com. Unfortunately, it appears that relatively few lawyers have filled out their profiles, so the site may not be of great value other than to confirm who has been selected.

There will be more discussion of a *Super Lawyers* listing in Chapter 3. For present purposes, if you find a suitable lawyer who is listed as a "Super Lawyer," make a note of that fact, and of the practice area in which the lawyer is so designated.

Best Lawyers in America. This guide has been published for twenty-five years. It claims to have a very sophisticated selection process and to be "the oldest and most respected peer-review publication in the legal profession." More information is available at http://www.bestlawyers.com. *Best Lawyers* is essentially a subscription model. As this is written, the book could be purchased on the website for $225 and online subscriptions cost $200 per year. The website allows free selected-lawyer searches but only if the lawyers or law firms have purchased links from the *Best Lawyers* website to their own law firm websites. Again, if a lawyer is listed in *Best Lawyers,* make a note of that fact.

More Specific Resources

Once you begin to compile your list, you will probably want to conduct more specific research on an attorney. Some of the general resources provided above can provide a lot of specific information, but there are also other resources that should be consulted for more detailed information.

Law Firm Websites. Almost every law firm has a website. Law firm websites vary considerably in their quality and the amount of information they provide. Some law firm websites provide an extremely limited amount of biographical information. Other websites provide complete biographical information, as well as publications, and sometimes even blogs and podcasts. My current firm has quite a comprehensive website, which can be found at http://www.ctflegal.com, with links to our blog and our podcasts.

LinkedIn. LinkedIn is a social networking site for professionals, located at http://www.linkedin.com. LinkedIn allows a user to post a detailed profile. Many lawyers are on LinkedIn. Some have posted detailed profiles, others have not. LinkedIn is growing, and more lawyers seem to be taking it seriously. As of this time, LinkedIn is hit or miss on information about lawyers, but it is worth checking. Some lawyers, I am told, have begun marketing on Facebook and other general social networking sites, but I do not use them for researching attorneys.

Google. Once you have the name of a particular lawyer you want to research, Google (as well as Bing and Yahoo) can be valuable. In "Googling" a lawyer's name, one can often find other information about a lawyer, sometimes including links to articles the lawyer has written or links to cases the lawyer has handled. The "advanced search" feature on Google can be useful in narrowing results.

Paid services. Two large subscription services provide access to all case law and many legal publications, as well as to news and information: Westlaw and LEXIS/NEXIS. It is possible to use these databases to search for cases that a lawyer has handled. Most business people, however, do not have access to these expensive resources.

Thus, I mention them as possibilities for deep research, but they are really not necessary to locate a good business attorney.

Conclusion

By using these resources, you should be able to compile a list, perhaps a large list, of potential business attorneys. In the next chapter, we will discuss how further to sift and evaluate the lawyers on your list. The goal will be to winnow the list down to several lawyers you will want to interview.

Chapter 2 Summary

- Lawyers are *not* fungible.
- You will probably want a business lawyer with a corporate law or commercial litigation background, or both, as your primary business attorney.
- Your ultimate task is to develop a list of at least three attorneys to consider as your primary business attorney.
- If you are in a small community, you may want to consider increasing the geographic scope of your search.
- Gather the information specified in the chapter in a systematic way. Use a spreadsheet or table to record and update the information.
- Many resources are available to find information on and ratings of attorneys, including *Martindale-Hubbell, AVVO, Super Lawyers, Best Lawyers in America* and *Chambers.* Many of these resources are free.
- Other resources available include law firm websites, LinkedIn, and information obtained through search engine results.

CHAPTER 3: EVALUATING THE INFORMATION

"It's called bat speed, and he ain't got it."

-Unidentified American League scout on Michael Jordan's unsuccessful attempt to play professional baseball, *Sports Illustrated,* March 14, 1994

If you have completed the spreadsheet using the resources discussed in Chapter 2, you should now have a fairly large list of potential candidates to be your primary business attorney. This chapter will help you determine which lawyers on your list have the legal equivalent of "bat speed," which I will call "legal intelligence."

Michael Jordan is one of the greatest athletes of all time, and probably the greatest basketball player of all time. His ability to hang in the air and body control seemed to defy the law of gravity. Nevertheless, even a great athlete like Jordan was unable to pick up a baseball bat and play another sport at the highest level.

Believe it or not, there is an analogy here to practicing law. Many highly intelligent people may have great abilities in other fields, but, for whatever reason, lack an outstanding aptitude for practicing law. Put another way, they may be accomplished generally or in other areas, but they lack high legal intelligence. Legal intelligence, as discussed in this chapter, is a combination of the raw ability to analyze legal issues, the ability to apply knowledge to legal issues, and experience.

This chapter will discuss what I look for to determine whether another lawyer has high legal intelligence. You will find that much of what follows consists of generalities. It is true that there is almost always an exception to every rule, and it is certainly true that every person is an individual with unique strengths and weaknesses. However, the purpose of this book is to help you find a good business lawyer to act as your company's primary counsel. In sifting through and analyzing the list of candidates you have developed, it is necessary to apply some general criteria that have proven valuable in finding good lawyers. Individual considerations can be left for the interview process, after the list has been cut down.

What follows is subjective and is, of necessity, a matter of opinion. I happen to believe that most accomplished lawyers would agree with these observations, or would at least agree they provide some meaningful guidance. However, lawyers being lawyers, I am also sure that other lawyers would apply the criteria somewhat differently, or might use other criteria. That said, here is what I look for in evaluating legal intelligence.

Raw ability to analyze legal issues.

The first component of legal intelligence is the raw ability to analyze legal issues. The most consistent indicator I have found for this component is success in law school. Although this may seem elitist, the simple fact is that the best law firms have always competed to hire people from the top of the class. Law firms, particularly large law firms, are very competitive environments. The firms assume that, by bringing in the brightest law school graduates, they are maximizing their chances of developing talented lawyers. It is true that not all will turn out to be suited for the law, but the chances increase with the best raw talent available.

It may surprise you to know that most business law firms *still* look to some degree at academic credentials even when they are considering hiring lateral candidates with years of experience. I have seen several experienced candidates turned down at least in part because their academic credentials just did not quite make the cut. This is not to say that academic credentials are the most important factor in choosing a business attorney. Of the factors in this book, it is probably the least important. But excellent academic credentials should be viewed as a positive factor in winnowing down your list. Here is what to look for in evaluating these credentials.

Class rank. Class rank in law school is one of the most Darwinian ways in which to assess raw legal talent. Although there is no hard and fast rule, I prefer to engage lawyers who graduated in the top 20 percent of their class. You have probably noticed in your research that, save for lawyers who graduated first or second in their class, most do not mention their rank. However, there are usually ways to determine this, or at least make an educated guess.

The *Order of the Coif* is a law school honor society with chapters at many (but not all) law schools. Membership is limited to the top 10 percent in the class. Thus, if a lawyer's resume lists the *Order of the Coif*, it provides an immediate answer to the question.

Lawyers will also sometimes list academic honors they received upon graduation. Although the system is not absolutely uniform among law schools, summa cum laude means that a person finished at the very top of the class. Magna cum laude graduates are just slightly behind, and cum laude slightly further behind. It is safe to assume that anyone receiving a cum laude or higher honor did very well in law school. Some law schools use different distinctions, such as graduating "with honors" or "with distinction."

It should be noted that some law schools do not use or release class rankings. There are various justifications offered for this, but the fact is that these schools deprive law firms and potential clients of important data.

The question will probably arise as to whether weight should be given to where a person went to law school. For example, should one assume that an Ivy League graduate has a high level of raw legal ability or should be evaluated more highly than a graduate of a solid state-supported law school? My answer is that it is generally more important *how lawyers did* in law school than *where* they went to law school.

This answer is based on working with lawyers from all over the country, but my experience in watching lawyers in the Atlanta market is illustrative. Atlanta has been an attractive market for law school graduates and lawyers for many reasons, including having a sophisticated level of practice in a more relaxed atmosphere than, for example, New York. Atlanta firms recruit heavily from the Ivy League schools and other top-rated law schools, including Virginia, Michigan, Vanderbilt, Duke, and the University of North Carolina, just to name a few.

However, the top two schools that Atlanta firms recruit from are the University of Georgia and Emory University (which is in Atlanta). For purposes of full disclosure, I went to UGA. UGA and Emory are both very solid law schools, consistently ranking well in the top quartile of law schools as ranked by the *U.S. News & World Report* annual law school survey (this survey, which has its proponents and detractors, does provide a good overview of law schools). Atlanta firms will also recruit from Georgia State University in Atlanta and Mercer University in Macon, Georgia. Georgia State is up and coming and Mercer is a well-established school, but both would rank lower in pure prestige than other schools mentioned in these paragraphs.

Although many Ivy League graduates do very well in practice, I have seen no discernable general correlation between *where* attorneys went to law school and their legal abilities. Certainly, the prestigious schools mentioned have produced great lawyers. So have UGA and Emory. So have Georgia State and Mercer. At my old firm, the Chairman of the firm is a very talented lawyer who went to the University of Toledo (Ohio) law school (ranked in "tier 3" according to *U.S. News*), and the Chair of the litigation department (a highly talented lawyer now general counsel for a publicly traded company) went to a law school that no longer exists! So again, although graduating from a prestigious law school is a good thing, *where* one went often matters far less than *how well* one did.

Law school activities. Certain law school activities tend to indicate that a person did well in law school. Foremost among these activities is participation on the school's law review or legal journal. A law review or journal is a publication consisting of articles, often by law professors, and often on esoteric topics. Students may author "notes," which are short articles, or "case notes," which discuss recent legal cases of interest. Getting on the law review is usually a competitive process that involves making good grades, a "write on" competition, or both. Participation on the law review is a credential firms look for when recruiting law students. If a student goes on to become an editor of the law review, that is another accolade.

It should be noted that most law schools have one or more secondary journals in addition to the front-line law review or journal. Many of the other journals involve more specific topics, such as international law. Although these journals can include fine articles and undoubtedly provide a worthy educational experience, the best students usually participate in the primary law review or journal.

Moot court competitions are another important activity. Students may win or place well in internal law school competitions, and then be selected to represent the school in competitions involving other schools. Being selected to participate on a moot court team or in a mock trial competition is an achievement.

Law school scholarships and honors. Receiving an academic scholarship is notable, particularly if it was kept through the final year of law school, as that indicates the student probably met academic achievement requirements for keeping the scholarship.

Law schools also issue other awards, which vary from school to school. One award issued at many law schools is an *American Jurisprudence* Book Award. *American Jurisprudence* is a legal encyclopedia, and many schools award the student who made the highest grade in a particular subject a copy of the volume of the encyclopedia for that subject. These and other awards should be factored into the analysis, but count less than the other issues mentioned previously.

You may be wondering whether a lawyer's undergraduate record should be considered. My answer is that generally it should not be for at least two reasons. First, it almost always takes a good undergraduate record just to get into law school. Therefore, stellar undergraduate credentials are not much of a differentiating factor. Second, as noted at the outset of this chapter, many extremely intelligent people do not, for whatever reason, have an aptitude for law. Excellent undergraduate credentials may well indicate general intelligence or aptitude in another discipline, but they are not typically indicative, in my view, of raw legal ability.

Before leaving the subject of academics, let me assure you that I am not trying to send you to a person who only thinks great thoughts and ponders obscure legal issues having no application to the real world. First, remember that academic success is only *one part* of the evaluation. Second, law practice is itself a business. It is highly unlikely that anyone without an appreciation for practicalities and dealing with others is going to have any long-term success in practicing law. Many of those who are purely academically oriented find their way into teaching or other lines of work.

The point is that if you can find a lawyer who is *really smart and* who meets all of the other qualifications, why would you not want to choose that person? Those lawyers are out there in virtually every community.

The Ability to Apply Knowledge to Legal Issues.

Applying knowledge to legal issues is perhaps the most important aspect of legal intelligence, but, in some respects, it is the most difficult to assess before actually working with a lawyer. There are, however, certain designations, awards and rankings that can help in making an assessment. In addition, the lawyer may have made presentations or written articles that may give an idea about how he approaches and analyzes legal issues. Finally, referrals and recommendations should be considered.

Martindale-Hubbell rankings. Martindale-Hubbell was discussed in the previous chapter, and you should have noted on your spreadsheet whether a lawyer has a rating and whether it is AV, BV, or "rated" (formerly CV). For many years, *Martindale-Hubbell* was considered the "gold standard" of legal directories. Not only was the directory comprehensive, its ratings were viewed as a valuable service. It should also be noted, however, that it had few competitors until relatively recently.

An AV rating has for many years been viewed as an accomplishment which many lawyers sought to earn and keep. In the past several years, however, there has been some controversy about *Martindale-Hubbell.* The company sells listings (historically viewed as a necessity by law firms) and they have become very expensive. A number of firms, including prominent firms, are reported to have dropped their *Martindale-Hubbell* listings. As of this writing, however, the vast, vast majority of lawyers and law firms appear in *Martindale-Hubbell.*

As for the ratings, I still generally look at an AV rating as a sign of some accomplishment. At the same time, I have dealt with a number of fine lawyers over the years with a BV rating, even though they are clearly in the upper echelon of attorneys. As noted above, many lawyers are not ranked simply because *Martindale-Hubbell* does not have enough information about them. Historically, rankings have been based on mailed surveys of lawyers and judges in the lawyer's community. It seems more difficult for corporate lawyers to obtain a ranking because they do not go to court and may, therefore, be generally less well known among judges and perhaps other lawyers. I thus view the lack of a ranking, particularly for corporate lawyers, as essentially meaningless and neither positive nor negative.

Martindale claims to be changing its ranking process (also adding a numerical scale) and to be re-ranking many lawyers. Only time will tell whether this is the right thing to do, or whether it will make the directory more or less authoritative. My personal opinion is that changing a time-tested formula may prove risky. Nevertheless, at present, *Martindale-Hubbell* remains a valuable resource. I use it frequently in researching other attorneys.

In considering the rankings, an AV rating is a plus. However, I would never engage a lawyer simply based on an AV rating. It is simply a piece of information that goes into the analysis. A BV ranking is neutral, particularly if the lawyer has not practiced for more than fifteen years. Having no ranking is also neutral because some lawyers, particularly corporate lawyers, have seemed left out of the process.

AVVO ratings. AVVO is a quite new and potentially valuable resource in finding an attorney. As noted in the prior chapter, however, an AVVO ranking can be dramatically affected by adding information to the bare bones profile that AVVO culls from public sources. Thus, I would generally consider an AVVO ranking in hiring only if the lawyer appears to have claimed and filled out his profile.

AVVO's algorithm is confidential, but it appears from my firm's experience that AVVO considers bar activities, speaking engagements, and publications strongly in ranking attorneys. Such activities can certainly lead to a higher profile in the legal community and are worthy endeavors. Such endeavors *may* also be indicative of expertise, though not always.

For example, most lawyers probably know other lawyers who are what I call "bar politicians," meaning they become highly involved in bar activities immediately out of law school and stay involved for the rest of their careers. Although some of these people are good attorneys, there are others who seem focused on simply gaining a higher profile.

Similarly, many excellent attorneys simply enjoy practicing law, and do not have time for speaking engagements (or perhaps, like many, shudder at the thought of public speaking) or bar activities. Accordingly, *if* an attorney has claimed and filled out his profile, a high AVVO ranking is another piece of information worth considering. However, if a lawyer does not have any bar activities, speaking engagements or publications, a ranking may understate a lawyer's ability. AVVO's own website is clear that its rankings should never be the sole basis for hiring an attorney.

Chambers. Chambers is not a publication that I generally use in hiring attorneys, although it was recently helpful in locating an attorney in the United Kingdom. *Chambers* seems to be, however, growing in influence and is an interesting publication. *Chambers* posts glowing commentary about its rankings on its website, which it says are based on a combination of lawyer submissions, client interviews, and independent research. *Chambers* says it has 100 researchers. Based on the short summaries on *Chambers'* website, the researchers largely seem to have been educated abroad (consistent with *Chambers'* international approach). Most appear to have no legal education.

In reviewing the selections for Georgia corporate and commercial litigation attorneys listed, I would agree that most of the attorneys selected are generally good attorneys, although there are a few I would not recommend and there are many omissions. *Chambers* also ranks firms in "bands" (from 1 to 6, 1 being the best). With respect to the Atlanta market, with which I am most familiar, many very good firms are included in the rankings, but I would not rank them exactly as *Chambers* has done. Particularly in its top rankings, *Chambers* appears to favor larger firms. Further, because *Chambers* appears to require law firm submissions, it should not be viewed as a survey of the entire legal community.

In sum, being listed in *Chambers* is another positive attribute. Full disclosure: My firm and I are not listed in *Chambers*, but we have not made a submission to be considered.

Super Lawyers. Law and Politics, in conjunction with local publications, lists "Super Lawyers" in certain states. The polling and ranking process is said to be rigorous. Only up to 5 percent of the attorneys in a state are included. As is the case with many services, *Super Lawyers* provides advertising opportunities to those selected.

My subjective evaluation of the *Super Lawyers'* selection process is that, as a general matter, those selected generally are accomplished attorneys. However, some excellent attorneys are omitted from the *Super Lawyers* list, some of whom I would personally rate higher than some included on the list.

One thing I like about the *Super Lawyers* process is that it is fairly open and does not appear to favor large firms over smaller ones. As is the case with *Martindale-Hubbell,* I can confirm that *Super Lawyers* actually does poll lawyers for recommendations. Because polling is involved, however, *Super Lawyers* is open to the criticism that it has aspects of a popularity contest. The bottom line is that, if someone is designated as a Super Lawyer, it is positive information. If someone is not on the list, however, that is not negative information, as there are omissions. Full disclosure: I have been included on the list of Georgia Super Lawyers for business litigation for several years.

Best Lawyers. Because of its proprietary model, *Best Lawyers* may be a resource that you do not want to use. If you use the free information on the website, be aware that it is not a complete listing as it includes only lawyers who have purchased links to their firm websites.

Best Lawyers is not a publication that I typically use to search for lawyers. My limited, subjective impression of *Best Lawyers* is that it is generally reliable in listing good attorneys, but that it misses many equally good attorneys. There is also an occasional selection that leaves me, at least, scratching my head. *Best Lawyers'* advisory board is composed largely of lawyers from large firms, and, again subjectively, the publication seems to favor lawyers from larger firms. If a lawyer on your list is listed in *Best Lawyers,* it is another positive sign. Full disclosure: I am not listed in *Best Lawyers.*

CLE presentations and presentations. Most states now require lawyers to take a certain amount of continuing legal education, or CLE. Lawyers take their CLE by attending seminars where other lawyers make presentations on various topics. Many lawyers view speaking at a seminar to be an honor and an opportunity to showcase expertise on particular subjects. Most lawyers who present at CLE seminars do have some expertise, so a history of presenting at seminars is another positive indication.

In addition, most seminars require presenters to prepare written materials. These materials can sometimes be found posted on firm websites or other websites. Reviewing these materials can give you some insight into a lawyer's analytical process, as well as his views on a particular subject.

Nevertheless, some lawyers do not have the time or inclination to participate in seminars, or may view seminars as "giving away" their expertise. Thus, the fact that a lawyer has not been a speaker or presenter should not be viewed as a negative indication.

Articles and publications. Many lawyers write articles, blogs, or even books to establish their credentials and expertise. As is the case with written seminar materials, articles and publications can also provide insight into a lawyer's views and thought process. Thus, publishing articles and publications is generally a positive indication. Many good lawyers, however, do not write for public consumption, so the fact that a lawyer is not published should not be taken as a negative indication.

Referrals and recommendations. Referrals and recommendations are usually positive and are certainly worth considering. In hiring or engaging other counsel for a client, I almost always seek referrals and recommendations internally at my firm, or from a select group of other lawyers whose judgment I trust.

There is a potential difference in the referrals and recommendations that I get from my sources and the ones you get from yours: Good lawyers are pretty reliable (and usually quite dispassionate) in judging the ability of other lawyers. On the other hand, if you are getting your recommendations from other business people, they may lack the experience to make an informed judgment, and may be basing their recommendation more on the fact that they personally like the lawyer than the lawyer's ability.

If you get a recommendation from a businessperson, try to get some more information. Here are some questions you may wish to ask (assuming the lawyer's name is Joe): What sort of work does Joe do for you? Why exactly do you recommend Joe so highly? What particular results has Joe achieved for your company that makes you so enthusiastic? Listen carefully to the answers. If the answers are detailed and make sense, then the recommendation should be viewed as a strong positive piece of information. If the answers are short and vague, take the recommendation with a grain of salt.

Experience

The third component of legal intelligence is experience. One might think that years of practice is the best indicator of experience. Certainly, years of practice can be an important indicator, but there are other aspects of experience that should also be considered closely.

Partner, associate, or "counsel." In looking at the resumes of lawyers, you will want to note titles, which are typically "partner," "associate," or "counsel." The titles will tell you something about the lawyer's place in the hierarchy of the law firm and may tell you something about the lawyer's experience. This section will discuss what these titles typically mean.

A partner typically owns a fraction of an equity interest in the firm and shares in its profits. In law firms structured as professional corporations, the equivalent position is a shareholder. Many large firms have adopted a two-tiered structure of equity and non-equity partners. The difference is usually based on the amount of business the lawyer controls and not on technical competence. In addition, most firms do not publicly distinguish between equity and non-equity partners. For purposes of finding a good lawyer, the equity/non-equity distinction is almost always meaningless.

In order to make partner, a lawyer usually has to have spent a number of years in practice and demonstrated qualities that make the firm want to keep the lawyer on the team. The number of years to partnership varies, but today a minimum of eight years out of law school is required at most firms in larger cities or with sophisticated practices, and that number can often be higher. Elevation to partnership, especially in today's economic environment, is far from a certainty. Partnership decisions depend on the firm's evaluation of many objective and subjective factors. In any event, the fact that a lawyer is a partner (or shareholder) is usually a positive indication in looking at a lawyer's level of experience.

Associates are lawyers who are employees of the firm. They can range from being straight out of law school to having quite a few years of experience. Senior associates are often the workhorses of a law firm: They are typically good lawyers with substantial experience and are able to perform at least most tasks on their own. In the past, many firms had an "up or out" policy, meaning that if an associate did not make partner after a designated number of years, he or she had to leave the firm. This sort of general policy, which is pretty stupid when you think about it, is no longer used by many firms. In addition, many firms, especially big firms, have extended the time to partnership. Thus, many highly experienced associates can be found at many firms. If a lawyer on your list is an associate, that is not necessarily a negative fact, but you will want to make sure that the lawyer has the necessary experience and is not too green to be your primary business attorney.

Some law firms use designations such as "Counsel," "Of Counsel," and "Senior Counsel." These designations can mean so many different things that they are impossible to define with any precision. At some firms, the Counsel or Of Counsel designation is used as a bridge from being an associate to making partner. At other firms, the designations are more permanent, and generally mean a lawyer who is experienced and respected, but not expected to make partner. At other firms, Counsel or Of Counsel can refer to a lawyer who is affiliated with a firm, and may work with the firm on certain matters, but generally has his or her own practice. Senior Counsel may be used for older lawyers who may have been partners, but who may want to cut back on their hours. There are certainly many other possible permutations. Because the Counsel designations can mean so many things, it is important to check on the lawyer's particular circumstances.

Industry expertise. In researching a lawyer's background, you may find that the lawyer has considerable experience in a particular industry or area of business. If your business is in this industry or business, this expertise may be extremely helpful. First, you will probably not have to spend time (and pay for the lawyer's time) in providing background information on your business. Second, a lawyer with industry expertise will probably already be familiar with some of the key issues faced by your industry. In fact, lawyers with industry expertise often prove to be a valuable source of business information for clients, helping clients keep abreast of business as well as legal issues potentially affecting their business. For these reasons, industry expertise, if you can find it, is usually a very positive attribute when considering hiring a lawyer. There are, however, some important caveats.

You probably do not want to hire a lawyer who already works for a significant direct competitor. One of my clients is preeminent in a particular industry. It competes with other companies, one in particular, for projects. It would be very awkward to try to represent my existing client and its main competitor. Representing clients inherently involves maintaining confidential information and usually involves advising the client in connection with business strategy. The old adage about the difficulty of trying to serve two masters applies with special force here. Similarly, if your business involves selling to certain regular customers, you would probably want to make sure that the lawyer does not already represent one or more of your most important customers.

Representative engagements. Many lawyer biographies will list representative transactions, litigation cases, or other experience. This information can be very useful in determining whether the lawyer's experience will suit your company's needs. First, the engagement may indicate industry experience, as discussed above. Second, the transactions may indicate whether the lawyer has experience representing companies of a similar size to your company. Third, the transactions may indicate whether the lawyer has experience handling the types of contracts or transactions that are part of your company's business.

If a lawyer on your list has representative engagements that fit with your business, it is a positive attribute. On the other hand, if the engagements seem very different than issues that affect your company, another choice may be in order. If a lawyer makes your final cut for an interview, you will want to follow up and ask more specific questions during the interview.

In praise of the generalist. Although experience in your company's industry or with matters that apply to your business is important, so is experience with a fairly broad range of legal issues. A good business attorney will be able to identify legal issues – many of which may never have occurred to you – that may affect your business. If an attorney has specialized in a narrow range of issues, that expertise can be extremely useful for particular matters. It is unlikely, however, that a specialist will have enough breadth of experience to serve as your primary business attorney. Although it is not a perfect analogy, a good business attorney functions somewhat like an internist or primary care physician does in medicine. Your business attorney should be able to handle most issues, but can refer you to a specialist when needed for particular issues.

In praise of the business litigator. In searching for a primary business lawyer, most lawyers would probably direct you solely to lawyers with a purely corporate law background: forming companies, drafting contracts, and handling mergers and acquisitions. Certainly, a lawyer with a purely corporate background may be a great choice. I am going to suggest, however, that you also consider interviewing at least one lawyer with some background in commercial litigation. Admittedly, having a litigation background myself, there is some bias in this suggestion.

Nevertheless, a person with a litigation background can bring skills and experience to bear that a purely corporate lawyer may not possess. Lawyers who practice general commercial litigation tend to handle a wide variety of business disputes. They tend to litigate about many types of contracts. They also litigate business torts, which are claims that do not involve contracts. In handling these types of claims, litigators are often adept at spotting risks that may arise in the future and that can be dealt with or lessened through planning.

It has been a pleasure over the years to work with many talented attorneys who practice purely corporate law. There are, however, two threads that tend to run through the way many purely corporate lawyers tend to look at things. First, purely corporate lawyers tend to put *complete* faith into contracts and documents. After all, that is their job, and having carefully crafted documents is, as noted in the first chapter, part of the Prime Directive and very important. In the relatively rare event of a dispute, however, purely corporate lawyers are often surprised when the documents do not *eliminate* risk.

Second, for reasons I honestly cannot fathom, purely corporate lawyers almost *always* overstate what can be achieved in litigation. They tend to tell clients that any dispute is winnable and will say something like, "We will get one of our crackerjack litigators to tear them apart." Some corporate lawyers also tend to lead clients to believe that the client will recover its attorney's fees in litigation, which is rarely the case. When asked to assist a corporate lawyer's client with a dispute, a litigator's first job is often to do a reality check. Good litigators also look for opportunities to resolve disputes early on, which can save clients considerable money, not to mention eliminating the business disruptions that always result from litigation.

It can be a little more difficult to find a business lawyer with a litigation background than a purely corporate lawyer. If you can find such people – particularly if they have access to excellent corporate help at the law firm – give them fair consideration.

Conclusion

By now, you should have enough information to have begun making significant progress in identifying your candidates for interviews. Here are a few final thoughts on this chapter. There are very few lawyers who are going to have every positive characteristic identified. You should expect, however, for a lawyer to have some of the positive characteristics, and if those positive characteristics have particular application to your business, so much the better.

In discussing many of the positive characteristics, I have commented that the failure to have that particular attribute should not be viewed negatively, and that is certainly true. If, however, in reviewing your assembled information about a particular candidate, you detected few or none of the positive attributes I have mentioned, then that candidate is probably one you will want to cut from your list.

Before making your final cuts, there is one remaining issue you will want to consider: Whether to favor lawyers from large firms or small ones. That topic requires its own chapter, and it is covered next.

Chapter 3 Summary

- Legal intelligence is to a lawyer as bat speed is to a professional baseball player.
- Legal intelligence consists of three elements: Raw ability to understand legal issues, the ability to apply knowledge to a legal issue, and experience.
- A lawyer's performance in law school is a good, although not perfect, indicator of the raw ability to understand legal issues.
- In considering law school performance, look at class rank, participation in important activities such as law review, and honors and awards.
- How someone performed in law school is generally more important than where someone went to law school.
- The ability to apply knowledge to a legal issue can be judged, to a certain extent, by recognition in publications such as *Martindale-Hubbell, AVVO, Super Lawyers, Chambers* and *Best Lawyers in America*
- Speaking at events such as CLE seminars tends to indicate expertise in a particular subject matter.
- Articles and publications can also demonstrate expertise in a particular subject area.
- Written seminar materials, articles and other publications can also provide insight into how the lawyer thinks and approaches legal issues.

- Length of time in practice is some indication of experience, but it is not the only indicator.
- A lawyer's position as a partner or shareholder in a firm is generally positive, but there may be talented associates and "counsel" you may want to consider.
- Industry experience is an important attribute; however, you should probably avoid lawyers who represent your major competitors or customers.
- Representative engagements can help you assess whether a lawyer's experience is consistent with your needs.
- Breadth of experience and the ability to identify legal issues – so as to be able to refer you to a specialist if needed – is also important.

CHAPTER 4:
LARGE, MEDIUM OR SMALL: ONE LAW FIRM DOES NOT FIT ALL

"Well, we have three sizes - medium, large and jumbo."

"What happened to the small?"

"There is no small. Small's medium."

"What's medium?"

"Medium's large and large is jumbo."

-Elaine and concessionaire, *Seinfeld*, "The Movie" (1993)

There is one particular issue that you should consider in narrowing your list of potential candidates: Should you choose a lawyer from a large, medium-sized, or small law firm? My general answer is that there is a lot of truth in the old adage that "clients hire lawyers, not law firms," meaning that the particular lawyer you hire is far more important than the size of the firm.

That said, there are some general considerations you may wish to consider in evaluating lawyers from different sized firms. I spent almost twenty-five years working in a large law firm environment, and then decided to switch to a much smaller firm. You might suspect that my current circumstances would cause me to favor smaller firms, but that is not the case. No law firm is the right firm for every client. In addition, law firms of the same size can be very different, so please take any generalizations in this chapter as just that: General tendencies that may or may not apply to particular firms.

"Big," "small" and "medium-sized" defined

As an initial matter, it may be helpful to define what constitutes a "big," "medium-sized" or "small" law firm. The answer appears to be about as clear as Elaine's experience with the concessionaire from the quotation at the beginning of this chapter. There is no accepted numerical definition (at least so far as I can determine), and, if you asked a group of lawyers, you would probably get many opinions.

In 2009, there were many postings on legal blogs about Fortune 500 general counsel sending work to "smaller firms" in order to save on legal fees in the tough economy. In reading the posts more closely, this actually seemed to mean the large companies were moving some work from the top 25 largest firms in the United States "down" to the top 75 to 200 largest firms. In other words, they were moving business from law firms with over 1,000 lawyers to law firms with, on a rough numbers basis, 400 to 700 lawyers. In my book, these are *all* "large" firms, just slight variations of the term. In addition to the different perspectives of extremely large companies (such as the Fortune 500) in comparison to smaller businesses, what is considered a "big firm" in New York City is probably a much different proposition than in, for example, Albuquerque or Little Rock.

Because most readers of this book will probably be owners or executives of small to medium-sized privately held businesses, I will try to look at law firm size from this perspective. From this perspective, I would break down law firm size in today's market this way: Large: 150 or more lawyers; medium: 50 to 149 lawyers; small: fewer than 50 lawyers. For the largest metropolitan areas, cutoff points would be a little higher, and for smaller cities, a little lower. One important caveat: In small towns, these numbers have little meaning because the largest firm may be 20 lawyers or fewer.

Large Firms

In conducting your research, you may have found a larger number of suitable candidates at large firms. If this is the case, it is not surprising. Almost all of the large, well-established firms have lawyers with excellent credentials. Large firms compete for the top law school graduates and will rarely hire lawyers without excellent credentials. Lawyers who have stuck it out and made partner at large firms are typically well-qualified.

As a product of having excellent lawyers, large law firms also, in general, do excellent work. Further, big-firm attorneys often have more opportunities than lawyers in smaller firms to work on sophisticated transactions or difficult lawsuits. This experience is very valuable.

There are also some particular types of business and legal work that favor using a big-firm lawyer as your primary business lawyer.

- If your company is a public company or is considering an initial public offering ("IPO") in the securities markets, you should strongly consider using a lawyer with considerable public securities experience. Most corporate lawyers with this expertise will be at big firms.
- If your company primarily does business with state or federal governments, you should strongly consider using a lawyer with government contracts experience. Many lawyers with this expertise will be at big firms.
- If your business is heavily regulated by a government agency, you should strongly consider using a lawyer with

experience in this area. Again, many lawyers with this expertise will be big-firm lawyers.

A claimed benefit of big firms is that they provide a "one-stop shop." In other words, your company may need access to legal expertise beyond that of your primary business lawyer, such as an environmental lawyer, an immigration lawyer, a patent lawyer, etc. Big firms often provide all of these disciplines under one roof. Similarly, if your company does business in multiple states, a big firm may have offices in most of the states in which you do business. Being able to access all of your legal services through one firm can be a convenience. There is, however, another side to this argument that is addressed later in the chapter in discussing small firms.

Big firms can also provide "cover" within a business organization. What does this mean? Think of the old IT adage: "Nobody ever got fired for buying IBM." If you are an executive in a business that faces a "bet the company" legal issue, you may want to hire a big firm. If things do not go as hoped, this may deflect any criticism that might be directed your way. Although this may not be an objectively valid issue when selecting the best available lawyer, we live in the real world, and, in the real world, cover is sometimes important.

At this point, you are probably thinking that you should restrict your search to big-firm lawyers. In fact, a big firm *may* be right for your company. There are, however, issues that might suggest a different approach, not the least of which is that the big firms do not possess a monopoly on great lawyers.

There are other concerns, but before going into them, let me say that they do not apply equally to all large firms. They probably apply, however, in some measure to most big firms and can be helpful to your overall understanding.

For many years, many large firms have practiced based on a "leverage" model. In order to visualize this model, consider a pyramid. The legal work comes in at the top (the partners) and is pushed down to the lower levels (junior partners, "counsel," and associates). In many large firms, a primary task of the partners is to keep the associates busy as the associates are not expected to bring in their own clients.

There are a number of potential consequences of this model. First, the lawyer that you *thought* you had hired may have little actual involvement in doing the work. Chances are that the first several drafts of a contract (or other document) will be done by a junior lawyer you have never met. Second, there may be multiple reviews of a document as it goes back up the chain and before it gets back to the partner for final review.

Many large-firm lawyers will try to defend this method as efficient and even cheaper by arguing that the work is done at lower hourly rates. Although the younger lawyers will have lower hourly rates, my experience is that this is rarely cheaper in terms of total cost because younger lawyers tend to be less efficient and the multiple-review process tends to involve many hours.

There are inherent factors in some big firms that have made the pyramid approach (or what also might be termed downward delegation) somewhat ingrained. First, large firms pay young lawyers extremely high salaries. Some firms pay first-year associates right out of law school $160,000 per year and may pay year-end bonuses on top of that. At least prior to the current economic environment, big firms justified large salaries and bonuses as necessary to attract "top talent."

Second, in order to pay for these salaries, many large firms impose high "billable hour" requirements on their associates of 1,900 to 2,200 billable hours per year (on rare occasions, even more).

A billable hour is an hour that is to be charged to the client at the lawyer's hourly rate. In order for associates to "make their hours," it is necessary to force the work down from the partners to the associates. Accordingly, the pyramid, the high salaries, and the billable hour requirements all feed each other in a circular manner.

The need to feed the machine also tended to mean less flexibility in fee arrangements. For many years, law firms increased the rates of all of their lawyers every year. Big-firm partners often have little flexibility in setting their hourly rates, at least without the approval of a committee. When I was at a big firm, the automatic annual rate increase was a source of some frustration.

For many years, it seemed that the big law firm model, with its strengths and weaknesses, would never change. Although there were periodic objections from clients and talk of alternative fee structures (see the next chapter for more information), most of it was just talk. Large law firms raised rates every year, the first-year associates' salaries escalated, billable hour requirements remained high, and the machine ran on, pretty much as described above.

The Great Recession *may* have thrown a monkey wrench into the big-firm machine. For "big law" as a business, 2009 was a year unlike any other. A number of prominent large law firms shut their doors. Many large law firms announced mass layoffs of associates. For the first time in my memory, many firms also laid off partners. In addition to announced layoffs, there were undoubtedly some "stealth" layoffs in which lawyers were quietly let go.

Big law firms are also facing new demands from clients. Many in-house lawyers, faced with their own company's financial issues and demands to reduce costs, have purportedly informed their law firms they will no longer pay for time on bills from first-year associates. Their justification is that they should not have to pay for training of new lawyers, particularly when they view the new lawyers as overpaid. Other clients, particularly those with large amounts of legal work, are demanding discounts or alternative fee arrangements. From a client's perspective, at least if you are a large client, it is currently a buyer's market.

It is a much more difficult question whether the current market conditions will lead to permanent changes in the way large law firms do business. To begin with, even after the layoffs, large firms remain structured as they always have been. There may be fewer lawyers, and perhaps relatively fewer associates and less leverage. But the associates that remain will still have to work and the downward delegation pressure is certainly still there.

Old habits die hard, and, assuming the economy improves, pressure from clients may lessen. My best guess – and it certainly could be wrong – is that any change at large firms will be generally incremental. A recent survey suggested that, despite a continuing difficult business environment, law firms intend to go back to raising hourly rates in 2010.

A few tips on how to deal with lawyers have particular application to large firms. When I hire a lawyer on behalf of a client, but particularly from a big firm, I try to avoid the pyramid problem by directly asking at the outset of the engagement: "*Who exactly is going to do the work?*" My assumption in dealing with a partner is that the work may be delegated. If so, I want to know *to whom* and to talk to the junior lawyer and review the lawyer's experience and credentials before proceeding with the engagement.

For the most part, I do not want work delegated down below a lawyer with at least four to five years of experience. Typically, the difference in savvy, understanding and ability between a fifth-year associate and a first-year associate is quite astonishing. In talking to the partner and the associate, I make it expressly clear that I expect the associate to be "my lawyer," and that I do not want to see any further delegation of the work to a less experienced attorney. I also make it clear that I intend to communicate directly with the associate and will check in with the partner as needed.

Even then, I try to follow the associate's first efforts very closely. It is usually pretty easy to tell whether the lawyer "gets it," is responsive, and is meeting deadlines. Although this will probably be a little bit more difficult for a businessperson, if you pay attention, ask questions when necessary, and trust your judgment, you probably will make good decisions. If I perceive a problem, I discuss it with the partner immediately and get another attorney assigned. Although this may hurt a young lawyer's feelings, that should not be a factor. You are paying for professional services from a large and prestigious organization, and that is what you have a right to receive.

Small Firms

Do not think we are skipping medium-sized firms. Medium-sized firms tend to be a mixture of the strengths and weaknesses of large and small firms, so it is easier first to contrast large firms with small ones.

Generally, small firms *may* provide services equal to or even exceeding those provided by most big firms. The two main questions are, first, whether the firm has high-quality lawyers, and, second, whether the firm has adequate resources to serve the needs of your business.

The previous chapters have provided you with the resources to assess whether a lawyer is proficient. In addition to the criteria discussed previously, significant big-firm experience is usually a plus. How much big-firm experience is "significant"? It certainly is more than having spent a year or two at a big firm. As a general guideline, perhaps five years would suffice. If a lawyer has been a partner in a big firm, that certainly qualifies.

Is big-firm experience a necessity? The answer is no, but you will want to determine whether the lawyer has experience handling sophisticated legal matters or at least legal matters of a type your business is likely to encounter. Almost every city has extremely well-regarded small or medium-sized firms, sometimes referred to as "boutiques." These firms perform work at a level equal to (sometimes better than) the big firms. If a small or medium-sized firm serves well-known clients, or if its partners have resumes rivaling those of big-firm partners, it is probably such a firm.

There are a number of reasons to consider using a lawyer from a small firm. Perhaps the main reason is personal service. Many small firms are not structured on a leverage model and there is more of a tendency for partners to do more of their own work or to be more directly involved in supervising it. Be sure, however, to check the relative numbers of partners and associates, which can usually be determined from the firm's website or *Martindale-Hubbell.* If there are four partners and fifteen associates, there will be the same leverage or delegating issue as there is in a big firm. Even if the firm demographics look favorable, you should still ask who is going to do the work in the interview. There are some small-firm partners who act just as if they were at a big firm.

A second and closely related issue to personal service is access. If your company is a small or medium-sized company that spends less than $50,000 a year on legal fees, the reality is that your company may be pretty far down the list of clients of a big-firm "rainmaker." This may mean that your calls are not returned as promptly as you would like, and it may also be difficult to get the services performed as quickly as you would like. To a small firm, however, your company would likely be viewed as an important client. If you have a legal issue that needs handling immediately, you may find you get a much prompter response from a small firm than a big one.

An important aspect of access often overlooked is that small firms tend to have fewer conflicts of interest than big firms. Before a lawyer can open a file on a new matter, it is standard procedure to run a conflict check. The purpose of a conflict check is to make sure that the firm does not represent the opposing party in the transaction or dispute. As a general matter, lawyers cannot represent one client in a matter that is adverse to another client.

Large firms, particularly ones with many offices, tend to have many conflict issues, and it can sometimes take a day or more to determine whether there is a conflict. I ran into conflict issues regularly when I was with a large firm, and the issues grew as the firm expanded and opened new offices. As a result, we had to send our clients elsewhere on several important matters and many smaller ones. Conflicts may still arise in a small firm, but they are much easier to check, and not as much of a problem. Do not underestimate this issue. If your company finds the perfect lawyer, it does not do much good if he regularly has to withdraw from handling your company's work because of conflicts.

A third reason to consider a small firm is cost. As a general rule, small firms charge less than big firms. In addition, again as a general rule, small firm lawyers have more flexibility to set their own rates and to agree to alternative fee arrangements (discussed in detail in the next chapter) than big-firm lawyers. Having this flexibility was an important consideration for me in deciding to leave the big-firm environment. Other lawyers moving to smaller firms have told me the same thing.

Small-firm lawyers would also argue that some of the claimed benefits of large firms are overstated. As noted above, large firms sometimes claim the benefit and convenience of having a "one-stop shop," with experts in various disciplines and perhaps offices in different cities. Small firms, by definition, will not have this capability.

Good small-firm lawyers would point out, however, that while all large firms have strengths, they are not equally strong in all areas. For example, a large firm's environmental department may not be nearly as strong as its general corporate department. Similarly, a large firm may have just merged with a firm in another city, and the lawyers in the new office may or may not be up to the standards of your primary lawyer. Lawyers at big firms are under considerable pressure to keep all of your company's work "in the house," if possible. This means they may refer you to less than the best available lawyer.

On the other hand, the small-firm argument continues, if your primary lawyer is with a smaller firm, and the firm does not have, for example, an environmental lawyer, the small-firm lawyer can refer your company to one or more of the best environmental lawyers in town without the pressure to keep the work internally. Similarly, if lawyers are needed in another city, the firm can affiliate with the best lawyers in that city without the constraint of using the firm's own office.

Which side of the argument about the "one-stop shop" is right? I would say that convenience favors the large firm. Large firms tend to have high-quality lawyers, and it is unlikely that you would be referred to anyone completely incompetent in another department or office of a large firm. On the other hand, getting the best-quality assistance and maximum flexibility may favor the small firm's argument.

Here are some circumstances in which you should consider a small firm:

- If your company is privately held, does not have stock that trades on the public securities markets, and has no immediate plans for an IPO;
- If your business does not regularly sell to federal or state governments;
- If your business is not subject to heavy government regulation;
- If you put personal service at a higher premium than being represented by a "name brand" large firm;
- If cost is a substantial consideration;
- If your projected legal fees are less than $100,000 per year ($50,000 in some markets).

It should be noted that, even if your company is publicly traded, sells to governments, and is subject to heavy government regulation, it *may* be possible to find a small firm that meets your company's needs. If a small firm claims to have such capabilities, you will need to check them carefully during the interview process.

Medium-sized firms

Having read the foregoing, you might conclude, somewhat like Goldilocks, that a medium-sized firm is "just right." Unfortunately, it is not that simple. A lawyer from a medium-sized firm may be "just right" for your business, but that may not be the case at all.

It is difficult to make any general comments about medium-sized firms as defined above because the definition covers a fairly wide range of scenarios. There is quite a difference between a firm of 50 lawyers and a firm of 149 lawyers. A firm of 50 to 60 lawyers is more likely to have the characteristics of a small firm, and a firm of 140 to 150 lawyers is quite likely to have the characteristics of a big firm.

Within the continuum, there are many variations. As law firms approach 100 lawyers, however, they have a tendency to become more like big firms. Such a law firm is likely to view big firms as direct competitors. It is likely that such a firm is managed more like a big firm (with multiple committees) and faces many, if not most, of the economic issues of a big firm.

There are many excellent lawyers in medium-sized firms. In considering a lawyer from a firm in this range, try to do more research on the law firm. Try to determine in the interview process (discussed later) whether the firm has more tendencies of big firms or small firms.

After all this, does size matter?

The outset of this chapter noted the old adage that "clients hire lawyers, not law firms." After all of the intervening discussion, this adage still holds true for most businesses. Most businesses can be well-served by a good lawyer in a large, medium-sized or small law firm. This is shown by the fact that clients tend to follow their lawyers when they move, for example, from a large firm to a small one, or vice versa.

There are certain companies, typically large, publicly traded companies or companies with governmental relationships or regulatory issues, that are probably better served by big firms. Even this statement, however, is a generalization. Most other businesses can be well-served by a good lawyer at any size firm.

The size of a law firm, however, may constrain a lawyer in providing services. Most of the issues are laid out in this chapter. These issues should be considered in your analysis, but the focus should be on finding the right lawyer.

Conclusion

By now, you should have the information necessary to cut your final list down to three to five lawyers to interview. If your business is like most, you may want to consider having lawyers from various sized firms on your final list. In the interview process, you will obtain more information to make your final choice. Before you begin interviewing, however, you need to be armed with some information about the always-important issue of legal fees, discussed in the next chapter.

Chapter 4 Summary

- The old adage "clients hire lawyers, not law firms" is true for most businesses.
- There is no accepted definition of large, medium-sized and small law firms, but, as defined in this chapter, large firms have 150 lawyers or more, medium-sized firms have 50 to 149 lawyers, and small firms have fewer than 50 lawyers.
- Large firms tend to have lawyers with good to excellent credentials.
- Because of the way they are structured, large firms tend to delegate down work to less experienced lawyers.
- If you are considering engaging a large-firm lawyer, it is important to find out who will be doing the work and to be satisfied with the answer.
- Large firms tend to be more expensive and less flexible in fee arrangements than small firms.
- The Great Recession has, at least temporarily, influenced many larger firms to be more flexible in their engagements.
- Large firms may be the right choice if your business is a public company (or is considering an IPO), if it sells to the government, or is heavily regulated.
- Large firms may provide a "one-stop shop" for specialists and other offices, but whether this leads to better legal services is debatable.

- Small firms may provide more personal service, but you still need to ask who is going to do the work.
- Small firms may provide greater access to small and medium-sized companies because a "little client" to a big firm is likely to be an important client to a small firm.
- Small firms may also provide greater access because they are less likely to have conflicts of interest than big firms.
- Small firms tend to have a lower cost structure and more flexibility than big firms.
- Medium-sized firms are difficult to categorize; however, as firms approach 100 lawyers, they tend to act more like large firms.
- For most companies, finding the right lawyer is more important than the size of the law firm.

CHAPTER 5: FEES: HOURLY RATES AND ALTERNATIVE FEE ARRANGEMENTS

"You know, the thing about you lawyers is that you are expensive. Tell me this: If I paid you $500, would you answer two questions?"

"Sure. What's your second question?"

-Author unknown, prospective client and lawyer in a bar (*circa, 1995*)

Any discussion of engaging a lawyer sooner or later turns to the subject of legal fees. Before turning to anything else, however, please remember the prime directive from the beginning of the book: *It is almost always more effective and less expensive to involve a lawyer earlier in the process than later.* This truly is the best advice I can give any business about saving money (not to mention heartache and angst) in the long run.

On the more immediate subject, let me acknowledge the obvious: lawyers are expensive. Further, fees probably are the main source of friction between clients and their lawyers. The reality is that there is no way for a business to get top-quality legal services without spending some money. That does not mean, however, that you should have to pay too much.

The best way to deal with fee issues is to put them on the table at the outset of a potential engagement. When I interview potential clients, it often surprises me that they do not raise the issue of fees. Knowing that fees are almost always an issue, I try to make sure we cover them if the client does not ask. The truth is that no lawyer – at least any good lawyer – wants fees to become an issue. This chapter will provide you with the knowledge to discuss the issue intelligently. Fees should definitely be covered in your interview process.

Hourly Rates

Background. For the nearly thirty years I have practiced, the hourly rate has been the standard basis for charging for business legal services. The concept is simple: The lawyer has a rate per hour, records the hours, and then multiplies the rate by the hours to establish a fee. Most firms bill monthly on this basis, although a few will bill quarterly.

There is no accepted standard hourly rate. Across the country, partner rates in all disciplines can vary from $150 per hour to over $1,000, and there are probably rates outside this range. As a general proposition, rates in large cities, particularly on the Eastern seaboard, the West Coast, and Chicago, are higher. Rates can also vary among practice areas. In general, the rates to defend routine tort litigation are lower. The rates for business and business litigation services are higher. The rates for certain specialties – such as some intellectual property work – tend to be higher still.

Rates also tend to vary depending on a lawyer's experience. Firms almost always charge more for partners than they do for associates, and each firm's rate structure tends to be based on experience, with some variations due to different areas of practice.

As stated, there is no set schedule for hourly rates. To try to give you some general guidance, however, I would say that as of this writing (January 2010) the range of hourly rates for partners for business and business litigation services in large cities generally range from $300 per hour to $750 per hour, with associate rates from $200 per hour to $350 per hour. The rates in New York City, Chicago, and California cities would generally be higher. The rates in smaller cities and towns tend to be lower. As you interview lawyers, you will get a better idea of the rate structure in your city or town.

For most of my career, hourly rates have crept up every year. Until recently, it was a normal event at most firms to increase rates at least every January 1. The economic difficulties of the past two years have, in some firms, at least temporarily changed this practice. However, recent news reports indicate that many firms are going to resume rate increases in 2010. To some degree, this is fueled by economic reality. The cost of running law firms is generally not decreasing, and many lawyers probably will face large personal tax increases after 2010. My best guess is, so long as the economy continues to improve or tread water, rate increases will resume.

Rate shopping. Many people have a tendency to rate shop among lawyers. Although you should try to find a lawyer with a reasonable hourly rate consistent with your business needs, I would urge you to be cautious in rate shopping for a number of reasons. First, although this may seem counterintuitive, there is *not* a clear direct correlation between hourly rates and the ultimate total cost of legal services. The reality is that some lawyers are far more efficient than others. Further, some lawyers are more aggressive than others about making sure they record every minute. A key factor can be experience. If a lawyer has experience handling very similar matters or transactions, it is likely that lawyer will take far less time than a lawyer doing something for the first time.

If your choice comes down to two lawyers with somewhat different rates (say $350 per hour compared with $400 per hour), my advice would be to put relatively little emphasis on the rate in your final decision. Consider other issues, particularly factors that bear on experience.

On the other hand, if your choice comes down to a very experienced lawyer with an hourly rate of $400 compared to a lawyer with essentially identical credentials with a rate of $650, then rate should be a factor in your decision. These types of differences will probably most typically be found in comparing large firms to small firms.

Asking for discounts. Another question is whether you should ask for a discount on hourly rates. Although you might assume you are proceeding under the old saying that "there's no harm in the asking," this is a potentially touchy subject from the lawyer's point of view.

Most lawyers have a standard hourly rate. This is the rate they already charge all of their clients, barring unusual circumstances. Many lawyers do not like the thought of charging a new client less than established clients who may have been with the lawyer for years. If a lawyer agreed to a lower rate and the word got out, it could cause trouble with established clients. The net result is that you should not be surprised if the answer is a flat no.

In considering asking for a rate discount, remember that a law firm is also a business. If you are going to ask for a discount, consider what you are offering in return. For example, you are far more likely to get a positive reception in asking for a rate discount if you are seeking general representation for all of your legal matters (and assuming that looks like a fair amount of work), than if you are seeking representation for one small piece of work. Similarly, if you have a large transaction or litigation matter that is likely to require a lot of work, you are in a better position to ask for a concession. You should also consider offering to pay a larger than normal upfront retainer (discussed below), or paying your bills especially promptly in exchange for a discount.

What I am about to say next may rub some readers the wrong way, but it is something you need to know. All lawyers have clients they view as their best clients. If lawyers practice long enough, however, they will run into one or more problem clients. Problem clients may complain about every bill, no matter how fair, or they may not pay their bills in the agreed upon period. Some problem clients pile on by trying to insist that their work be put ahead of everyone else's, no matter the circumstances.

Lawyers, especially good lawyers, will fire problem clients. More often, good lawyers will turn down business if a prospect shows signs in the initial interview of becoming a problem client. If you ask for a large rate discount, particularly without any apparent justification, do not be surprised if you are turned away.

Dealing with the delegating down issue. In the discussion of large firms in the preceding chapter, we discussed the issue of work being delegated to associates. Clients often face the argument: "Yes, our partner rates are high, but most of the preliminary work will be done by an associate with a much lower rate. I will review the final product and make sure it is fine, which will result in a much lower cost to you."

Do *not* just accept this argument at face value because, in practice, it often does not hold true. You should ask who is going to be on the team performing your work, you should review their credentials, and you may wish to insist on meeting each person before proceeding with the engagement. You will want to know whether the younger lawyer regularly works for a partner or is assigned to the partner. Lawyers who work together regularly tend to be more efficient than those who do not. Sometimes, you will be told there will be a large team of people handling your work. As a general rule, the larger the team working on your project, the greater the expense. Although there are some matters that require a large team of lawyers, most matters can be handled by one or two lawyers.

Do not assume that the delegating down issue is limited to large firms. You should always ask who is going to do the work regardless of whether you are talking to a lawyer from a large, medium-sized, or small firm. You will gain a lot of information by asking this question.

Is the hourly rate system going anywhere? Over the years, there has been a lot of criticism of the use of hourly rates. The primary criticism is that the system encourages inefficiency. Simply put, the longer something takes, the greater the fee. It is also argued that the hourly rate system puts all risk of inefficiency on the client. These criticisms have a great deal of validity.

The counter-argument is that the hourly rate system, compared with other billing approaches, allows a client to purchase just what it needs. Thus, if a matter is quickly resolved, the client gets the benefit. There is some truth in this as well.

The bottom line is that the hourly rate system is probably here to stay for at least the indefinite future, and at least for certain types of work. During my years in practice, there have been periodic surges of criticism of hourly rates and calls for reform. The level of criticism has never been higher than during the economic crisis of the past two years.

The hourly rate system, however, is a stubborn thing. There are articles about clients who try other options and revert back. There will be other options (some discussed below), but I suspect the majority of business-related legal services will be performed on an hourly rate basis.

Alternatives to Hourly Rates

There are alternatives to the hourly rate model. Although alternative models have existed for years, the issue has come to the forefront in the Great Recession. According to news reports, many firms, including large firms, are entering into more alternative fee arrangements than ever before.

You may wish to explore alternative fee arrangements when interviewing your candidates. This section will cover some of the more common alternatives, but your candidates may have other suggestions. Please keep in mind that fee arrangements may be regulated by state bar rules, which may impose limitations or conditions on certain arrangements.

The best alternative fee arrangements offer something to both the client and the lawyer. In discussing alternative fee arrangements with a lawyer, keep the win-win concept in mind. It should be mentioned that some of these arrangements are more likely to apply to dealings with your regular business attorney (the subject of this book) than others.

The flat fee. Many clients do not like the billable hour approach because of its inherent uncertainty. Simply put, you do not know what the bill will be until it is received. This makes planning and budgeting difficult. The flat fee provides an answer to this: The law firm agrees to do a fixed scope of work for a fixed price. The firm does the work and you pay the bill (although you should expect the firm to ask for a substantial upfront payment).

The flat fee has many virtues: It adds certainty for the client and is simple. It places the risk of an overage on the law firm, not on the client. A flat-fee arrangement should virtually eliminate disputes over bills.

The potential difficulty with a flat fee is not in concept but in the execution. First and foremost, a flat fee requires a clear and defined scope of work. The scope will need to be defined in an engagement letter and signed off on by the lawyer and the client. Any assumptions that govern the work should be clearly stated.

Why is scope so important? A flat fee is pretty much like an agreement with a builder to build a three-bedroom house from a set of plans for a set price. If you ask the builder to add a fourth bedroom, a finished basement and a sunroom, you will get change orders and you will pay more.

Certain types of work are more amenable to a flat-fee arrangement, such as corporate or LLC formations, sales agreements, nondisclosure agreements, form terms and conditions or leases. Experienced lawyers can usually determine the effort that should be required in performing this type of work and quote it on a flat-fee basis accordingly.

Do not overlook the possibility of combining different types of fee arrangements. For example, if your company is contemplating entering into a series of complicated, but similar, transactions, you might consider agreeing that the initial transaction be done on an hourly rate basis. Presumably, the first transaction will require the most work and the most interaction with the attorney. After the initial-transaction documents are finished to your satisfaction, it may well be possible to handle subsequent similar transactions for a flat fee per transaction (which should be substantially less than the fees spent on the first transaction).

Other types of work are not so amenable to a flat-fee arrangement. For example, most firms would be reluctant to quote defending a civil litigation matter for a fixed fee. The reason is that there is no certainty to litigation. Litigation might be settled in the first month or it might go on for years. Similarly, lawyers in litigation cannot control what the other side will do. The other side might be particularly difficult in filing every conceivable motion or serving every conceivable discovery request. Because of the uncertainty and lack of control, most firms will probably not consider flat fees for business litigation, at least on a general basis.

On the other hand, it may be possible to handle *parts* of litigation on a flat-fee basis. Affirmative aspects of litigation, such as preparing a complaint, or preparing affirmative written discovery requests, could be performed on a flat-fee basis, with other aspects being performed on an hourly rate basis.

The contingency fee. The contingency fee is one of the oldest forms of alternative billing arrangements. This arrangement applies when a party has a claim against another party. The concept is simple: The lawyer agrees to prosecute the claim in exchange for a percentage of the recovery. The percentage is usually between 33 and 40 percent of the recovery. If there is no recovery, there is no fee.

The contingency fee has been used for years in personal injury litigation. Contingency fees have been used far less often in business litigation but are probably gaining in popularity. The contingency fee reduces the cost of prosecuting the claim to the business to virtually nothing (but see discussion of out-of-pocket expenses below). In exchange for taking the risk, a good contingency-fee case gives a lawyer a chance to recover well in excess of standard hourly rates.

Despite the increasing use of contingency fees in business cases, you may find it difficult to find a lawyer willing to take a case on this basis. The lawyer will need to be convinced that there is a substantial chance of winning, there are substantial damages, and, if successful, the defendant or its insurance company can pay the settlement or any judgment. Many business cases involve claims back and forth between two businesses with exposure to both sides. In such circumstances, a good lawyer would be reluctant to take a case on a contingency, as it is not likely to involve a large recovery.

Reduced hourly rates with a partial contingency fee. This approach is a combination of the hourly rate basis and the contingency fee. Again, this approach only applies if the client has a claim against another party. Under this approach, the firm agrees to a substantial reduction in its standard hourly rates, but with the stipulation it will recover a contingency fee if successful. Instead of the usual 33 or 40 percent contingency fee, it might be reduced to 20 percent. The rates and the percentage are both subjects for negotiation and agreement.

From the client's perspective, this type of arrangement lessens the out-of-pocket cost while the litigation is pending. In addition, if the litigation is successful, a smaller percentage of the recovery is shared with the law firm than in a straight contingency fee matter. From the law firm's perspective, the risk of a straight contingency fee is substantially lessened and the firm knows that it will receive at least some compensation for its efforts. A firm may thus be willing to take a case on a partial contingency basis that it would not take on a straight contingency fee.

Problems can potentially arise with contingency and partial contingency fee matters if the client decides midstream that it does not want to pursue the matter. The law firm may therefore insist on a provision in the engagement that requires the company, upon deciding not to pursue a claim, to pay an amount that would bring the billing to the firm's standard hourly rates. All of these issues can and should be discussed and agreed to in advance if possible.

Reduced hourly rates with a success fee. In many instances, a company may wish to pursue a merger, acquisition, or business transaction that will have a substantial value to the company if successful, and little value if not.

Assuming the legal work is substantial, some firms may be willing to take such a matter on a reduced hourly rate basis with a success fee. This is an arrangement similar in concept to the reduced hourly rate and partial contingency basis discussed for litigated matters. The firm agrees to a substantial reduction in hourly rates while the transaction is being handled. If the transaction closes, the firm receives a success fee in an amount greater than if it had taken the matter on a regular hourly rate basis.

There are several potential advantages to this approach. First, the client benefits by paying substantially less while the legal work is being performed and reduces its costs if the matter is not successful. Second, the company and the firm both have a financial interest in pursuing the matter to a successful conclusion. Third, from the law firm's perspective, such an agreement provides an opportunity to beat its standard hourly rates if successful.

Of course, there are caveats. A law firm may be more likely to enter into such an arrangement with a long-term client – one with a good track record – than a new client. Because the benefit to the law firm is achieved only if there is successful conclusion, the firm will want to make sure that the client earnestly intends to pursue the transaction and has the means to see it through. The firm will also want to investigate the transaction thoroughly and determine that there is a reasonable chance of success. Again, the firm may insist that there be a provision for increased payment if the client later declines to pursue the matter or if the transaction fails for other reasons (*e.g.*, lack of financing) attributable to the client.

Out-of-Pocket Expenses

In addition to whatever arrangement is made regarding legal fees, you will be expected to pay out-of-pocket expenses. Law firms differ in out-of-pocket expenses charged to clients, but they may include copies, long-distance telephone charges, travel expenses, postage, courier charges, and computerized legal research charges. In litigated matters, out-of-pocket expenses will include court filing fees, court reporter's fees, investigative fees, and videographer's fees. Out-of-pocket expenses are usually included on the monthly bill.

In the instance of large charges, the client may be requested to pay them directly.

Sometimes, matters will involve the charges of other professionals, particularly in litigated matters. These charges may include fees and expenses for accountants, computer forensic experts, electronic discovery vendors, and expert witnesses.

In terms of engaging a business lawyer for most common needs (litigation excluded), out-of-pocket expenses are probably not a huge consideration. Nevertheless, because many readers may be unfamiliar with how law firms work, the subject is worth mentioning.

Conclusion

Legal fees are a subject you should discuss at the outset of any engagement. Many business people seem to avoid this discussion, perhaps because they do not know what to expect. In conducting your interviews, which we will discuss in the next chapter, you should freely discuss the subject of fees. This chapter should have provided the information you need to discuss the issue in an informed manner. As you conduct your interviews, you will gain a better understanding of the hourly rate structures and related issues that prevail in your community.

Chapter 5 Summary

- Legal fees should be addressed directly and at the outset before hiring an attorney.
- The most common basis for hiring a lawyer is on an hourly rate basis.
- Hourly rates vary considerably across the country. In larger metropolitan areas, a range that would currently (as of 2010) cover most business and business litigation attorneys is $300 to $750 per hour for partners and $200 to $350 per hour for associates.
- Hourly rates alone are not a good indicator of final cost.
- Experience in handling matters similar to yours is an important cost consideration.
- Relatively small differences ($50) in hourly rates should usually be ignored in engaging an attorney.
- Significant differences in hourly rates ($100 or more) should be considered in conjunction with other factors.
- Do not expect firms to discount hourly rates simply by asking.
- If you ask for a discount, consider adding a reason for asking, such as a promise of a substantial amount of work.
- Flat fees can be a good alternative for routine or predictable matters.

- Flat fees can sometimes be used for part of the work, with the remainder handled on an hourly rate basis.
- Contingency fees can sometimes be used for claims in business litigation, but they are often not suitable.
- Reduced hourly rates with a partial contingency can more often be used to handle business litigation claims.
- Reduced hourly rates with a success fee can be considered for transactional matters.
- Regardless of the fee arrangement, you will be expected to pay for out-of-pocket expenses.

CHAPTER 6: INTERVIEWING THE CANDIDATES

"Nothing is more difficult, and therefore more precious, than to be able to decide."

-Napoleon Bonaparte

The next and final step in finding your business lawyer is interviewing the candidates and making a decision. This process is not substantially different from any job interview. This chapter will give you insight in how to set up the interview, conduct it, and to evaluate the responses. At the end of the day, however, my advice is to use your instinct. By now, you should have assembled a list of several candidates, any one of whom would probably at least be adequate. You know more about your business than anyone else. You know more about how you prefer to interact with people than anyone else. In choosing the best candidate, your first instinctual choice may be the best.

You may wonder whether you can handle the interview process over the telephone. The answer is of course you *can* handle the interview over the telephone, but why would you want to? After all, you are trying to find a professional with whom you hope to work closely on important matters affecting your business. You will be paying for the lawyer's services and may end up spending considerable time with the lawyer you choose. It just makes sense to take the time to interview the candidates in person unless they are far away.

Setting up the Interview

Although it might be tempting to summon the candidates to your office, you should avoid this urge. Visiting a lawyer's office is going to give you important clues about how the lawyer practices. You will probably be able to observe, for example, how the lawyer interacts with subordinates and whether the relationship appears comfortable and positive.

In setting up the interview, telephone the lawyer's office. On rare occasions, you might be put through directly. The chances are, however, that you will have to deal with a secretary or receptionist as a gatekeeper. Here is what to do: Tell the person you are speaking to who you are, what your position is, and that you are in the process of trying to find a lawyer to handle your company's business. Tell the person that you have done some preliminary research, that the lawyer appears well-suited and that you would like to set up a meeting. If someone referred you, you should use that person's name.

If the lawyer is in and is not immediately occupied, you may well be put right through. Of course, the secretary or receptionist may need to take a message or put you through to voice mail. Whether leaving a message with a person or on voice mail, state slowly and clearly who you are, the name of your company, and that you are looking to engage a lawyer as the company's counsel. If your name is not a common one, spell it. Then state that you would like to set up a preliminary meeting at the lawyer's office lasting 30 minutes to an hour within the next week. Then clearly and slowly leave your telephone numbers.

The foregoing may seem pretty obvious and basic to you. Apparently, however, it is not to many people. I cannot tell you the number of calls I have been asked to take when the person does not identify himself or why he is calling. Sometimes I take the call, but, more often, I direct them to voice mail. At law offices, we get the same trash calls from telemarketers and others as you do at your business, and we value our time just as you value yours. If you announce yourself clearly and state why you are calling, it is not only polite, it helps us to respond.

Once you connect with the lawyer, again state who you are, who your company is, and why you are calling. Expect for there to be some banter back and forth and for the lawyer to ask some preliminary questions about you and your business. Here is an important caveat: Discuss general business all you want, but do *not* discuss at this time any confidential matters. It could create a bad situation for you and the lawyer if the lawyer's firm is already representing an adverse party.

At some point during the call, you should expect to cover information for a preliminary conflict check. If the lawyer does not mention it (some lawyers do not check conflicts until further in the process), you should. The firm will check its records regarding your company and regarding any adverse or potentially adverse parties. "Adverse" is a term lawyers use in this context, but it simply means anyone on the other side of a lawsuit or a potential transaction, or who has direct interests that differ from yours. This is also the time to cover whether the firm represents your key competitors, any companies that you regularly do business with, or anyone else antagonistic to you.

To raise the subject of conflicts, you should say something like: "I understand that conflicts of interest are a big issue with lawyers. Would you please run our company through your database before we meet just to make sure that the firm has no matters that are adverse to us?" You should also mention any subsidiaries or affiliated corporations, especially if they use unique names. If you know of any adverse parties for a particular transaction or litigation, you should name them, as well as the names of any known owners or principals of any adverse companies. Then, you should say something like: "Our key competitors are X and Y. I would like to know whether you represent or have represented those companies when we meet. Also, we regularly do business with A and B, and will need our lawyer to help us in our business dealings with those companies. Could you check those as well?"

Ask the lawyer to report back to you directly or through an assistant regarding the results of the conflict check before the meeting. If there are any current direct conflicts (*e.g.*, the firm already being adverse to your company), politely decline the meeting (if the lawyer has not already) on the basis of the conflict. As far as conflicts with competitors or your customers, you may want to take the meeting and inquire further. An isolated representation (particularly if it is finished) with a competitor or customer is generally not a reason for concern. If the firm represents competitors or customers regularly, you may want to decline even the initial meeting.

Assuming all goes well, set the date and time for the interview. Then repeat the process with your other candidates to set up additional meetings.

Should You Expect to Pay for the Initial Meeting?

Some lawyers charge for an initial meeting or consultation. In my view, *if* the purpose of the first meeting is an interview about whether to hire an attorney, you should not expect to be charged. Quite simply, lawyers should bill their clients, and, at this point, you are not a client.

There can be, however, exceptions and gray areas. For example, if a company representative and I have spoken at some length on the telephone, we have cleared conflicts, and the representative has indicated he wishes to engage our firm's services, my assumption is that I have been engaged, and subsequent meetings are about business and on the clock. To avoid this issue, make it clear that the meeting you are requesting is about whether to engage the lawyer and his firm.

Another issue arises when the prospective clients abuse the initial meeting. The meeting should be about the client's needs, the lawyer's experience, and whether the possible relationship appears to be a good fit. Some prospective clients step over the line and try to get "free" legal advice about their specific immediate problems. If you step over this line and particularly if the meeting lasts for several hours, the lawyer may assume that you have decided to make the engagement and may send you a bill. Depending on the circumstances, that may be fair.

If you follow the guidelines above and keep the meeting to between 30 minutes and an hour, you should not be charged. Most lawyers, particularly good lawyers, view initial meetings as an opportunity and part of their business development efforts and will not charge for them. If you are concerned about it, cover it in the telephone call when you are setting up the meeting.

The Meeting

It is a simple thing, but make every effort to arrive on time. Lawyers frequently have their day booked with activities, and, if you are late, it may affect how much time the lawyer can spend with you.

Either in the initial telephone call or early in the interview process, you should explain that you have already done a considerable amount of research on the lawyer's background and are familiar with his educational background and achievements. You should explain that you are interested in using your time in the interview to discuss the lawyer's experience and how it relates to your business, and how the lawyer typically works with clients.

Here are the subjects you should definitely cover:

- If not already covered in the telephone interview, you should cover some of the key points of your business (again, not confidential information). Do not be surprised if the lawyer already knows a lot about your business, having conducted research on your website or the Internet. If the lawyer is prepared in this way, and particularly if he asks incisive questions, that is a positive indicator.
- Ask the lawyer to tell you, without revealing confidential information, about any experience the lawyer has in connection with your business or industry. You may have some information from your own research, but this will give the lawyer a chance to expand and give you more information.
- If you know the types of services you will need, discuss the lawyer's experience in providing such services.
- Ask *how* the lawyer does his work. This is where you cover the delegation issue. Here is one way you can ask the question: "I have heard that a lot of lawyers simply send work to the younger lawyers in the firm, and the client ends up with a bill with almost all of the time on it from people he has never met. How do you handle work?" Listen carefully to the answer, as it will tell you a lot. You may get the "we try to make sure that work is handled by people with the most appropriate hourly rate" answer that was discussed earlier. If so, ask precisely *who* would assist on your work and ask to meet them. Ask whether the younger lawyers regularly work with the candidate. Ask how and when the candidate becomes involved and what is done to ensure quality.
- Ask directly about hourly rates and fees. Ask how billing is done. Ask whether the firm uses any alternatives to hourly rates and what they are. Ask whether the firm will do some

work on a flat-fee basis, and, if so, what types of work it will handle for a flat fee. Ask about other arrangements as may be appropriate.

- If everything has gone well, you may wish to ask for references. You should be aware, however, that any references you are given will undoubtedly say good things about the firm.

Evaluating the Performance

Chances are that, following the meeting, you will have one of three reactions: (1) "Wow! That person was impressive"; (2) "He seems to know his business and would be able to do the job"; or (3) "I just don't think I could ever work with that person!" If your reaction is No. 3, you should probably cross the lawyer off your list immediately. Otherwise, make note of what you learned and your impressions in your spreadsheet.

Here are some things you should consider in your evaluation:

- Was the lawyer enthusiastic about the prospect of representing your company? This may seem a bit subjective, and perhaps even trite, but you want your lawyer to be concerned about your company and looking out for you. It can be very important.
- Was the lawyer prepared for the meeting? Had the lawyer taken the time to learn something about your company? If the lawyer took the time to prepare well for the meeting, chances are he will perform well on the job. Preparation is also another measure of enthusiasm.
- Was the lawyer a good listener? If there is one personal characteristic that good lawyers seem to have, it is being a good listener. Did the lawyer pay attention when you were talking? Did the lawyer ask sensible follow-up questions to

draw more information out of you? Was the lawyer a good conversationalist?

- Did the lawyer answer your questions directly? Is this a straightforward person? Contrary to lawyer jokes, the best lawyers are usually very direct and honest people. How did the lawyer respond to the delegating question? Did you get a direct answer or did the lawyer sidestep the issue? How comfortable and direct was the lawyer in discussing fees?
- Did the lawyer's answers provide more detail on industry expertise? Does the industry expertise seem truly relevant to your business?
- Did the lawyer's answers provide more detail on experience in handling the types of legal issues your company is likely to encounter?
- Did you like this person? This is an important question. You do not need your lawyer to be your best friend, but it sure helps to have a positive relationship. First impressions tend to govern how we feel about a person later, so they should not be ignored.

Making the Choice

If you have come this far and done the research and conducted the interviews, congratulate yourself. You certainly have more information than the vast number of people looking to hire a business attorney. My bet is that you will have a pretty good idea of who you prefer. If not, try to be dispassionate. Look at the data again. Consult with your colleagues. You may want to ask for a short second interview and bring a colleague.

If the choice comes down to two or three lawyers who all seem good, go with your first instinct, as it is probably the right choice. You should also remember that, in engaging a lawyer, you are not committing yourself to a permanent relationship. If you use the lawyer and things do not work out, you can always go elsewhere.

In that regard, do not burn bridges with the other candidates, but tell them of your decision (no one likes to be left hanging). In telling them, you might want to consider saying something like: "I was very impressed with you and your firm. Right now, I am going to try the other firm, but I may well be back if it doesn't work out."

The Engagement

After you make your choice, the lawyer should confirm the relationship. Typically, this is done with an engagement letter, although some firms may have a different practice. Bar rules may require particular procedures or provisions in an engagement letter, so practice may vary from state to state.

Especially for new clients, it is a common practice to require a "retainer," which is simply an upfront payment or a down payment. Lawyers vary in their practices regarding retainers. Normally, I will ask a new client for a retainer in an amount sufficient to cover anticipated fees and expenses for the next 30 days, but circumstances can change this. Retainers are usually applied against bills and the balance is to be paid by the client. In certain circumstances, particularly if there is concern about the client's ability or willingness to pay, an attorney may require an additional retainer as a condition of continuing the representation. If a client is an existing client with a good record of paying its bills, I normally do not ask for a retainer for further work.

My personal approach is to try to keep an engagement letter as simple and straightforward as possible. My engagement letters typically cover: (1) the scope of the representation (*i.e.*, what the firm has been hired to do); (2) the financial arrangements, including any retainer required, the hourly rate, if applicable, and the client's responsibility for out-of-pocket expenses; (3) how the client will be billed (typically, monthly); (4) the client's responsibilities regarding bills (to bring any questions or issues forward within 30 days, and, absent such issues, to pay within 30 days); and (5) in the unlikely event of any dispute, that the matter will be resolved by binding arbitration.

An engagement letter establishes a contract between the client and the law firm. If the lawyer sends an engagement letter that you do not like or do not understand, *bring up the issue or question immediately.* Discuss your concerns with the lawyer. If needed, ask the lawyer to send a new engagement letter superseding the old one. As is the case with almost anything, if an issue is discussed and resolved quickly and in a straightforward way at the outset, it will rarely become a problem later.

Conclusion

Sometimes, business people have difficulty deciding important matters, including engaging a business attorney. If you have followed the steps in this book, you will already have far more information than most people looking to hire an attorney. If it comes down to a difficult choice, go with your first instinct.

Chapter 6 Summary

- Plan to meet with your prospective candidates in person.
- Schedule the meeting at the lawyer's office.
- When you call to set up the meeting, announce who you are, your company name, that you are looking for company counsel, and that you wish to speak to the particular lawyer.
- Before the meeting, have the lawyer run conflict checks regarding your company, any adverse parties, as well as any key competitors or key customers.
- Expect the meeting to last 30 minutes to an hour.
- You generally should not expect to pay for an initial meeting before you have decided whether to engage the lawyer.
- At the meeting, focus on the lawyer's industry experience and experience in handling legal matters similar to those you anticipate.
- Be sure to ask the delegation question, and how exactly your work will be handled.
- If the lawyer indicates he does delegate considerable work, ask to meet the lawyer or lawyers who would be expected to handle the work.
- Discuss fee issues openly and get a clear understanding of how the lawyer and the law firm charge for their work. Ask about alternative fee arrangements.

- Your initial reaction following an interview is important. If you just cannot see yourself working with this candidate, take the candidate off your list.
- A lawyer's enthusiasm for representing your company and level of preparation for the meeting can be important gauges of whether the lawyer is right for your business.
- A hallmark of good lawyers is being a good listener.
- Consider whether you like the lawyer. A lawyer does not have to be your best friend, but it is good to have a cordial relationship.
- If making a choice seems difficult, be confident in your information and instincts, and remember that you are not committing to a permanent relationship.
- Once you make a decision, the lawyer should confirm the representation with an engagement letter, which should clearly spell out the scope of the engagement and the financial terms.

CHAPTER 7: MAKING IT WORK

"Coming together is a beginning; keeping together is progress; working together is success."

-Henry Ford

Having chosen an attorney, the next challenge is making the relationship work. The most rewarding and beneficial attorney-client relationships are when your attorney becomes an integral part of your team: a trusted adviser and resource who can not only help keep your business out of legal trouble, but can help your business succeed. There is no magic formula for establishing such a relationship; however, this chapter will offer some thoughts on how to make it work.

Tell the attorney exactly what you want to accomplish from a business perspective. This idea is so simple but is so often overlooked. Sometimes, a client will have been to another attorney, have talked to an attorney at a cocktail party, or done some background reading. These clients think they know what they want, so they will come in and say, "I need to form an S corporation," or something similar. Some clients will actually be quite insistent about what needs to be done, apparently believing that cocktail chatter or the Internet is a better source of information than the professional they have just engaged. Interestingly, the greater education clients have, the more likely they are to take this approach.

The reality is that most clients do not know what they need. Some clients may have a good idea of what they need but may be unaware of better alternatives. Here is a better way to approach the situation noted above: "I am starting a new business and think I need to form a corporation or some sort of entity. I want to make sure my personal assets are protected and that the tax burden is as low as possible. One lawyer I talked to informally suggested an S corporation, but I am not an expert, and I need your advice."

Hopefully, the lawyer will steer the client to possible alternatives even if the client is insistent. Some clients, however, are incredibly stubborn, bringing to mind the old adage, "You can lead a horse to water, but you can't make him drink." Do not be one of those clients. Make your business objectives clear and let the lawyer provide the legal advice.

Involve your lawyer in planning your strategy for a transaction. Many clients treat their lawyers as if they were a fire alarm: Use only if needed and in the case of an emergency. Other clients want to use their lawyers only as a scribe: Someone to write up the business deal they have already made. I have seen a number of European clients tend toward this approach, which can be particularly dangerous since they often lack a detailed understanding of the U.S. legal system.

Using a good business lawyer like a fire alarm or as a scribe, in the United States at least, is quite simply a bad idea. Good lawyers are used to being involved early on in transactions and discussing the legal options in conjunction with the client's business objectives. These planning sessions are usually very useful and help familiarize the lawyer with the business objectives and the client with possible legal options, obstacles or constraints. These sessions may last a long time, and, yes, you will in all likelihood be charged for them. However, they help eliminate false stops and starts and glitches, and they usually lead to a smoother transaction, where all the options have been thoroughly considered.

Allow your lawyer to learn about your business. The best relationships I have with clients occur when I get to know the ins and outs of the client's business and learn the client's preferences as to how to do business. These types of relationships only fully develop over time, but there are things that can be done to move them along.

For example, if your company is a manufacturer, giving your lawyer a plant tour is usually well worth the time. It is difficult to explain, but seeing how a company operates in person is much like a picture: It's worth a thousand words. Tours also provide an opportunity to ask questions. Understanding the details of how work is done and the problems employees encounter on a daily basis often leads to better legal solutions. If a tour is not possible, perhaps there are sales or training videos the lawyer can review.

Understanding a client's market can also be very important. This issue was likely covered to some degree in the interviewing process. Now that you have engaged the lawyer, providing a deeper understanding can be helpful. Similarly, understanding a client's strategic plans and objectives can be important in serving a client.

Over time, there is a cost-saving component in educating a lawyer about your business. You do not want to have to educate a new lawyer about your business every time a legal issue arises. Further, once a lawyer understands how your business works and your preferences in connection with doing business, the lawyer can simply handle the matter with less need to discuss every detail with you.

Be direct and expect your lawyer to be direct. If you are discussing an issue with a lawyer, get to the point and be direct. If you are embarrassed about something, remember that the attorney-client relationship is, with very few exceptions, confidential and privileged.

Also remember that experienced lawyers have probably heard similar stories before.

Assuming, as is most often the case, you have nothing to be embarrassed about, it still helps to get to the point sooner rather than later. You should also expect and allow your lawyer to be direct. For example, if you say, "I'm planning on getting together with my main competitor tomorrow and we are going to discuss pricing and dividing markets," you should expect a very quick and direct response from your lawyer not to do that, as your company could be sued and you could end up in jail. Sometimes, lawyers have to tell you things you do not want to hear. In such instances, do not adopt a "shoot the messenger" mentality. Discuss why the news is bad and what the options are.

Do not play lawyer. Some clients adopt a variant of the know-it-all approach. These clients, however, do not initially come to their attorneys with preconceived notions. Rather, these clients may work with the lawyers on one or two transactions and then come to think that this lawyer stuff seems pretty easy. In a misguided effort to save time or money, they decide they can handle the next transactions themselves, perhaps trying to reuse the documents from the previous transactions.

Often, these attempts at playing lawyer are caused by a desire to save money. In this regard, please remember the Prime Directive from the beginning of the book. Spending a little to get something right in the first place is almost always cheaper than trying to clean things up on the back end. There are probably provisions in the earlier documents that were added for the peculiar circumstances of that transaction. There may be considerations in the new transaction that need to be addressed. Even a fairly simple document, such as a nondisclosure agreement, often needs to be tailored for particular circumstances.

If your business has a number of very similar transactions, ask the lawyer whether he would consider doing subsequent transactions on a flat-fee basis. Even if you stay on an hourly rate basis, subsequent transactions should cost less than the initial transaction, because the lawyer will usually just be making adjustments to the prior documents. Those adjustments, however, can be very important, so you should let the lawyer make them.

Do not edit the facts. Some clients want to present a very limited set of facts to a lawyer. Again, this tends to be fueled by the notion that this will save money and the thought that it will prevent the lawyer from "wasting time going down rabbit trails." This is just another version of playing lawyer. The chances are that you do not know all of the facts that might be relevant to a legal issue. Further, clients sometimes seize on particular facts they *believe* to be relevant, but are not.

Give the lawyer all the facts. If you are not sure facts are relevant, err on the side of giving too many facts rather than too few. A wide-ranging opening discussion of a situation with your lawyer may well lead to better alternatives that would otherwise not be apparent. Your lawyer is not a mushroom to be kept in the dark.

Do not lie or hide the ball. One would think this would be obvious, but most of us have probably heard the lawyer joke about how you tell when a lawyer is lying (his lips are moving). Comedians (and, to some degree, the media) foster the notion that the best lawyers are a little slick, sleazy or underhanded. Perhaps the myth about lawyers leads some clients to believe that they should lie or hide the ball with their own lawyer.

The worst thing a client can do is lie to a lawyer, and, for the record, most lawyers are very honest people. In my experience, outright lying by clients has been exceedingly rare. Sometimes, however, clients will "hide the ball" and not reveal important facts because they are embarrassed or because they want to protect a business associate, friend, or relative. Again, it is hard to help someone without knowing all the facts.

One final word about lying or hiding the ball: It is deadly in litigation. Trial lawyers have an old adage that is very true: "You lie, you lose." In addition, courts have become much less tolerant of failing to produce relevant documents and information during the discovery process in litigation. Disclose everything to your attorney, and let the attorney decide whether it must be produced. If you overlook something or stumble upon a misplaced file, tell your lawyer immediately.

Review the relationship periodically. As is the case with any relationship, it is good to review your company's relationship with a lawyer and a law firm from time to time. Some law firms have adopted formal client-evaluation programs. My preference with regular clients is to have a meal or informal meeting "off the clock" periodically. Regardless of how it is done, the important thing is to get any concerns out on the table and deal with them in a constructive manner.

If there is something you do not like about the way a lawyer has handled something, or if you believe ongoing matters could be handled more efficiently, bring it up. If there is a member of a lawyer's team you just do not like, ask for a change. If you would like an alternative billing arrangement, put it on the table. From the lawyers' perspective, we all want happy clients, and it is much better to have a chance to fix something than to wake up one day and receive a call that the client has decided to move to another firm.

Handle billing and payment issues professionally. If there is one issue that arises more than any other between lawyers and clients, it is billing and payment. Hopefully, you will already have discussed billing in detail during the interview process, and the lawyer will have covered the basic procedures in the engagement letter.

As noted above, my standard engagement letter states that clients will raise any questions or issues regarding billing within 30 days of receiving the invoice. This seems like a reasonable procedure, and I cannot recall a client objecting to it. Regardless of whether your lawyer has a similar procedure, raising any billing questions promptly is just a matter of common sense.

When you receive a bill, you or someone in your company should review it promptly. If the engagement is based on hourly rates, the bill should be itemized. This means there should be a brief description by the timekeeper (the lawyer or legal assistant doing the work) for every time entry explaining what was done and listing the time spent. If a bill is not itemized, you should call immediately and ask for an itemized bill.

Time descriptions are an art and not a science, and some lawyers are far better at it than others. In my view, a time description should tell you succinctly what was done. As an example, if a lawyer were reviewing an insurance policy in connection with a matter, the entry "file review" would not, at least to me, be sufficient. The entry "review insurance policy in connection with possible coverage issues" would be sufficient, because it concisely explains what was done.

What you want to look for in reviewing an itemized bill is whether it provides a concise summary of the work done in the prior month, so that you have a reasonable understanding of what was done, what progress is being made, and what you are paying for. If the bill does not provide this, call your lawyer and discuss it. You may be satisfied with the explanation, or you may want to ask for a revised bill.

Assuming the descriptions are adequate, you will want to look at the time spent in relationship to what was accomplished. Does anything seem out of line or excessive? Be reasonable in your assessment. You should remember, for example, that drafting documents almost always requires several rounds of revisions to produce an acceptable final product. I cannot recall ever writing a contract or brief, or even a letter of any substance, that did not require at least a couple of rounds of edits and revisions.

The simple truth about hourly billing is that some things take more time than expected and some take less. As an overall guideline, when reviewing the bill of another law firm for a client, I try to determine whether it appears fair as a whole based on the work that is described.

If you believe you have been overbilled, you need to bring the issue to your lawyer's attention immediately. Tell the lawyer you have some concerns about the bill and want to discuss them. You might want to discuss your issues in person. In any event, you will want to discuss the concerns when you both have a copy of the bill in front of you. Have a frank but polite discussion. The lawyer may be able to address your concerns to your satisfaction or may agree to adjust the bill.

If the bill appears in order, *pay it.* Most law firms expect to be paid within 30 days. Most law firms are small businesses, and cash flow is as important to law firms as it is to any business. Law firms have to pay rent, payroll, and other bills, just like every company. If your company policy requires longer than 30 days to pay, that should be negotiated up front as part of the engagement.

Law firms vary in how aggressively they follow up about past-due bills. With the recent bad economy, law firms have been more aggressive in their collection efforts than previously. Even if a law firm does not follow up aggressively, you should never assume that the firm does not notice. All firms review receivables regularly, and most firms put considerable pressure on partners to keep their receivables up to date.

What are the consequences of not paying? Many firms may give you a little more time before your past-due account becomes an issue. At some point, however, the law firm is going to stop doing work for your company. The law firm may require that your company pay its past-due bill and pay another retainer (probably substantial) before doing more work. If a matter is in litigation, the lawyer will likely file papers asking to withdraw as your company's counsel. Finally, it is possible that the firm will sue your company to collect. A lawsuit, however, is the unhappiest of endings for all concerned, but it should never come to that.

Conclusion

The best attorney-client relationships are those where the lawyer becomes a key member of your company's team. A good business lawyer can and should become a valuable and trusted resource in helping structure your business transactions. If you follow the advice in this chapter about how to deal with your attorney, you should be on the way to a long-term and mutually beneficial relationship.

Chapter 7 Summary

- Tell the lawyer what you want to accomplish from a business standpoint in a particular transaction or matter.
- Involve your lawyer early in the strategic planning for the transaction.
- Help educate the lawyer about the details of your business through methods such as plant tours or videos about your business.
- Be direct and expect your lawyer to be direct.
- Do not "play lawyer."
- Do not edit the facts when discussing a transaction or matter with your lawyer.
- Do not lie or hide the ball under any circumstances.
- Review your relationship periodically.
- Handle and resolve any billing issues promptly and professionally.

INDEX

S

Made in the USA
Charleston, SC
11 May 2010